Enjoy!

M. Fred

July 2018

# A DAY IN THE LIFE OF A COUNTRY VET

**Fred Newschwander DVM**

**2018**

**With Illustrations by Maggie German**

# CONTENTS


INTRODUCTION .......... vii
TOMMY .......... 1
SOFT AND WARM .......... 6
WHAT'S FOR DINNER .......... 9
SONNY .......... 13
THE NIGHT VISITOR .......... 19
HEY DOC, CAN YOU CUT MY HORSE .......... 22
A LONG WALK HOME .......... 25
EYE SEE YOU .......... 30
MOTHER'S LAST RIDE .......... 33
GONE FISHIN' .......... 37
THE HUNT .......... 40
NICE KITTY .......... 44
GOOD STEW .......... 47
DO YOU BELIEVE IN MIRACLES .......... 50
NICE MOMMY COW .......... 55
HAS ANYONE SEEN MY HORSE .......... 58
FREE PUPPY .......... 63
YOU CAN'T KEEP A GOOD MAN DOWN .......... 67
THE PRINCESS .......... 71
HE DID WHAT .......... 74
WHAT TOOK YOU SO LONG .......... 77
HERE KITTY KITTY .......... 81
HERCULES .......... 84

DOC ........................................................................................88
MR. ROGER'S NEIGHBORHOOD .....................................92
BEDTIME STORY ....................................................................97
NO HITCHHIKING ALLOWED .........................................101
THE WELDED COW ..............................................................106
PHONE HOME ........................................................................111
THE OLD SWIMMING HOLE .............................................114
IN THE BERRIES ...................................................................117
CARPET BAG KID .................................................................120
BAD STUFF SOMETIMES HAPPENS (TO VETERINARIANS) ...........................................................123
VIGNETTES ...........................................................................127
A 'MOSTLY TRUE' STORY ............................................131
POPCORN TURKEY ..........................................................134
HOW THE ANGEL GOT ON TOP OF THE CHRISTMAS TREE ....................................................................................137
AFRICAN HORSE SAFARI ...............................................141
THE FABLE OF THE COYOTE'S TALE ..........................149
PLANKED CARP RECIPE ..................................................152
ACKNOWLEDGEMENTS .................................................155

# INTRODUCTION

How do you answer life's age old question: what to do with your short sojourn on this planet? Adolescence is a struggle just to discover who you are and how you *fit in.* High school should be a time to establish a foundation for life or to prepare for higher education. You can follow a tradition of a family trade, profession, or business. Some have known that "they always wanted to be a _____," while others, unfortunately, have grappled and never found a satisfying occupation. I, too, pondered what to do with my life, but in a fortuitous moment of inspiration, saw my future laid out before me.

I grew up on a small irrigated hobby farm in the Sonora desert area of central Washington. Sports, mountaineering, horses, and working to earn money for college expenses were my main extracurricular activities through high school. My parents were both educators so higher education was an obvious default for my future. I was a valedictorian, lettered in football and baseball, did well on college board exams, and thus earned a scholarship to Wesleyan University in Connecticut.

I *bucked* baled hay by the ton for a summer job during the 1950's and this money (effectively about \$6/hour at a time when the minimum wage was \$.75/hour) with the scholarship, enabled me to fund my own education. Between working to earn money for college, sports, and my outdoor hobbies, I had little time to *hang out* or *get into trouble* during high school and so off I went on a 12-hour 3000-mile \$96 flight from home to New York. Prior to that, I had never ventured outside of the state. I had always planned to get a PhD in mathematics but found I was competing against classmates who were true geniuses. If they got an A grade on an exam that left me in the B category and I felt I couldn't compete. So, I decided that an advanced PhD degree in mathematics was not going to be a good fit. My father was a PhD chemist, so as a fall back, I completed a fifth year at the University of Washington taking 4 chemistry courses.

This was the peak of the Vietnam War and the military draft was in effect. The selective service board said I was *goofing off* by getting a second BS and thus I lost my 2S military educational deferment. That and my low draft lottery number sealed my fate. 50 years later I attended a university reunion and found that out of 200 male classmates all but about 10 moved on to advanced degree programs thus retaining their 2S educational deferment and avoiding the military all together. The other 10 all enlisted in the Navy via OCS.

This was the moment of my life changing realization. Chemistry had been a better fit than mathematics, but now I had the military to deal with. One afternoon while sailing a small dingy on Lake Washington I suddenly realized that I wanted to be a veterinarian. However, military service was going to be a huge obstacle to my plans for the future. The draft was even going to pull me out of class in the middle of spring quarter, so I called the state selective service director and said, "I know you've *got me*, but isn't there some way for me to finish the quarter and not lose the money and credits?" He said, "Well son, it looks like we have *got you*, so what you need to do is ask for a change of induction site and that will delay the paperwork long enough for you to finish the quarter."

I got 100% on the Army induction exams in Seattle, so they did their best to convince me to train for an officer's commission at the Army Officer Candidate School at Ft Benning, Georgia, but this meant a three-year commitment instead of two. So, I told Uncle Sam, "No thank you." Having two degrees, knowing how to type, and possessing poor eyesight and a previously broken neck from college football, I assumed I would not end up digging fox holes. So, I was shipped off to Fort Ord, California and the reception center. They kept me there for almost a month trying every day to convince me to attend OCS and promising me a branch transfer from Infantry branch to Chemical Corps because of my chemistry background. I continued to decline the offer and marked the passing days off on my calendar.

During this period, to help fill the slowly dragging hours, I wrote daily letters to my girlfriend. In one I said, "Someday, I'm going to have to ask you if you really do want to marry me." She wrote back saying, "YES! WHEN?" I never did ask her to marry me but happily our plans went ahead anyway. How foolish we were to decide to marry during such an uncertain period of our lives. Realizing the difference in quality of life between being a married officer and married NCO (non-commissioned officer), I finally agreed to go to OCS. I had been previously told that because of my neck injury, I could probably avoid the draft altogether but it seemed like an unpatriotic thing to do. Now I was locked into three years before my life's plans could resume.

Five years of university education, three years in the Army as a staff officer, one year of pre-vet studies, four years in veterinary school and finally, at the age of 31, I began what was to be a fascinating 38-year career as a mixed animal veterinarian.

How many people are fortunate enough to be able to say that, if they could go back and have a *start over*, they would choose the same career path? I wish I could have reached my endpoint a little sooner but I would gladly do it all over again. You don't get a *mulligan* on life.

# MY DOG PIPER

**My best friend, footwarmer, trail buddy, alarm clock, dish washer, unpaid assistant, burglar alarm, muse and proof reader. One of the major drawbacks to owning Border Collies is that they are often more intelligent than their owners.**

# TOMMY

I guess you could call Tommy handsome. He was a black super-sized shorthair with a white tuxedo vest and four white spats. Long white whiskers were a striking contrast on his black face. However, his voice was not exactly what you would call sweet and melodious. When he wanted something, it was even a little bit demanding and annoying. He had gotten rather long in the tooth and claw and the ground was sneaking up and getting closer to his belly. His age definitely showed, and in terms of life expectancy, he was surely as old as his owner Amanda Green, but he had a swagger and an air of confidence that discouraged any dogs in the waiting room from having a staring contest. However, in spite of his great attitude, he was losing weight because his kidneys were wearing out. They were throwing protein away faster than he could take it in.

I had provided veterinary care for Tommy for many years when Mr. and Mrs. Green brought him in for appointments. We had parties for *tutoring*, vaccinations, deworming, abscesses, ear mites, and dentistry. The Greens were in their late 80's when Mr. Green died. Tommy's job suddenly became much more critical for he was the continuity between Amanda and the happy memories of her earlier days. I had little doubt that he slept on her bed or her lap and kept her day occupied by yowling for attention and demanding special treats. The Green offspring lived in distant cities, and Amanda had outlived most of her friends so his companionship was especially important.

My heart sank when I saw her walk through the door carrying Tommy. Her hair was a little disheveled and her face mirrored her inner anxiety. Tommy meowed unhappily and his right rear leg hung at a twisted awkward angle. Amanda explained that he often slept on a sunny southern exposed inside windowsill. She had heard a thump, an audible snap, and then a shriek. She looked to see Tommy hobbling on three legs. He had landed clumsily and broken his tibia. Us old folks don't always land on our feet. Cats in chronic kidney failure lose weight and their calcium metabolism may be disrupted. His bones had become thin and brittle and unable to withstand even a fairly routine stress. The worried look on Amanda's face mirrored her inner turmoil. We got some pain meds on board, took an X-Ray and sat down to discuss our options.

"He's so old. Do you think we need to put him down?" By then, however, the drugs had kicked in and Tommy was feeling no pain and was purring and seemed quite comfortable enjoying chemical euphoria and all the attention.

With a smile on my face I told her my old platitude that "If you put a cat together with all his broken bones in a room and come back in three weeks he will probably be walking around complaining about the poor room service." The healing won't be perfect but will be functional and the cat will be fine.

I suggested, "I don't think Tommy is an acceptable anesthetic risk but I think we need to give him a chance. Let's try a Thomas Splint." Imagine putting your broken leg through a padded ring up to your crotch. Rods run from the ring down the front of your leg to the ground and then up the back of your leg to the ring. When you try and bear weight on the leg, the rods, which are slightly longer than your legs, transfer the load from the ground past the fracture up to your pelvic bones. A little more sedative, some carefully bent and shaped splint rod, a lot of white tape with a *Smiley Face* drawn on it with black marker, and Tommy went home to sleep it off. Progress reports indicated Tommy was managing fine if a little awkwardly. "I had to move my best chair to Tommy's favorite sunny spot in the dining room and he meows whenever he needs to be lifted up or down. I think he is actually enjoying being an invalid for all the attention he gets from me," said Amanda.

Six weeks passed and it was time to take the splint off. We heard the engine cough when the old tan Chevy coupe expired in the parking lot. I knew Tommy and Amanda were there when I heard the tap, tap, tapping of his splint clunking on the tile floor of the reception room. Tommy purred while I removed the tape holding the splint on and in no time his now scrawny leg was revealed. Tommy stood up and stretched……. and his leg collapsed. There had been no healing at all. The calcium imbalance caused by his kidney failure and prevented all functional bone metabolism. Amanda sat back and said, "I guess we made the wrong choice. It looks like it must be time." I was about to agree until Tommy rubbed up against her face.

I thought for a moment and said, "Tommy got around so well even dragging that heavy awkward splint that I think he would do fine on three legs. But we still have the anesthetic risk and recovery to consider." We discussed all the pros and cons and decided to give Tommy another *last chance*.

I decided to do the surgery that day during my lunch hour so we would have the afternoon to observe and assist in his recovery. With appropriate fluids and pain meds the surgery went quickly and smoothly. It didn't take long to destroy what nature took 18 years to produce. We took the leg off in mid-thigh so there wouldn't be a stump that Tommy might be tempted to *peg* around on. However, recovery was not going well. Tommy's liver was also 18 years old and between the kidneys and liver he wasn't clearing the anesthetic. He was hanging on but barely. I called Amanda and gave her the grim news. "Well, if we are going to lose him, I guess I want to be there." We dejectedly put her in the rocking chair in the office with Tommy in her lap and I checked in on them whenever I had a break between appointments. It didn't look promising.

Amazingly however, every time I peeked through the door, Tommy seemed stronger. For all intents and purposes, we had given up on him but he wasn't nearly ready to quit. I sent Amanda home to rest, promising to call her if there were any changes. When I checked on him late that evening, Tommy was failing again, and so I called Amanda. "I'll just take him home with me so he won't be alone when he goes." I dreaded the sound of the phone the next morning.

The next dayI knew what the news would be when Cindy, my receptionist said, "Amanda is on the phone."

Amanda cleared her throat and said thankfully, "He's better and even drank a little milk." We changed the dressing that afternoon and although Tommy looked like something the dog dragged in, there was a little flicker of light in his eyes as he licked Amanda's hand.

As the days passed, Amanda discovered that whenever she put Tommy down, or left him alone for a while, he weakened, but as long as she was with him, especially if she was holding him or had physical contact, he got stronger. She got an old apron with a pocket in the front, put a diaper in the bottom and carried Tommy with her wherever she went. His head just poked out over the top of the apron pocket .The fuzzy cat basket had the place of honor on her bed on the side where her husband used to sleep. Three weeks later Tommy led Amanda back in the office front door on his leash to have the stitches removed. She appeared to be dressed in her *Sunday best*, had a brilliant smile on her face, and had her long gray hair tied neatly in a bun. Tommy was definitely back and ready to meet the challenges of his daily life.

We saw Tommy periodically for the next few years for routine checkups. He was long past the age when he needed any vaccinations. We tried to schedule appointments for late in the day so we would have time to chat and reminisce with Amanda and catch up on what had been going on in Tommy's and Amanda's life. She explained that if the weather was pleasant, Tommy liked to sleep in the rose bed outside the living room window and sometimes was able to ambush a foraging mouse which he proudly brought in for Amanda to admire. Birds stunned after hitting the window were also easy prey. He even trained her to scratch his right ear because he was lacking the necessary equipment. Looking slightly embarrassed she said, “I found a small old wicker baby carriage for Tommy to ride in so he can come along if I go on a longer walk. You should see the startled look on people’s face when they look in to see my *baby*.”

Almost three years later on a rainy Sunday morning, the phone rang again. It was Amanda. “Tommy and I had a quiet evening last night and we watched the game shows on TV, but he didn’t wake up this morning. I thought you would want to know.”

About two weeks later I called Amanda. “We have an abandoned kitten someone brought in to the clinic and we don’t have enough kennel room. Could you foster it for a few days until we find it a permanent home?” We never did find a permanent home for that kitten. He was black with a white chest and four white spats. We had named him TJ for Tommy Jr.

**Berta**

# SOFT AND WARM

Peter Beck was a dairyman in British Columbia, Canada. He had emigrated with his father as a small boy from Holland. They were drawn by the economic opportunity and the wide-open spaces of western Canada. Canada welcomed the settlers for their skills and work ethic. Through hard work and frugality, they had prospered and had a 100-head purebred Holstein Friesian dairy herd. The fences were painted white, the pastures were clipped, the barn trim was a contrasting color, and they were the envy of all the dairymen in the neighborhood. They even washed their tractor. They felt right at home in the lowlands of the lower Fraser Valley with its seasonal rain and frequent flooding.

It was hot, hot, hot. 95 degrees F or 35 degrees C in Canadian. Humidity was……. steamy. We were sweating through the last of the appointments when Judy said, "Dr. Fred. Peter Beck is on the phone." He had just started milking and wouldn't be finished for 3 hours.

He said, "Berta, my best producer, is calving and I can't get to her. Can you come out?" I mumbled something rude under my breath and said I would be right out. I pulled my sweaty scrubs off over my head and pulled on my coveralls, zipped down to the waist to try and keep cool. No AC in the work truck so I used the 440-cooling system: 4 windows down and 40 miles an hour.

She was gentle and huge: 1400 lbs. or 635 kilos in Canadian. Her dark eyes were soft and kind and drops of sweat glistened on her pink nose. Pete had her locked in a holding pen so I slipped a cow halter over her head and tied her to a strong corner post. She stood there contentedly still chewing her cud, belching, and wondering what all the fuss was about. I don't know if she liked being scrubbed down behind with cold water but it sure felt good to me. I lubed up and reached into the birth canal to see, or I guess I should say feel, what was going on. Everything seemed normal with the head and both front feet presented. I had to jerk my hand back out when I got bit by the as yet unborn calf. I laughed at myself and fortunately no one had been there to see my foolishness. Reaching in again but more cautiously, I determined that the calf didn't seem too large so I thought I might be able to pull it by hand without using the calf puller. I put a chain and hook on each front leg and started pulling, and pulling, and pulling. I was about to give up and get the calf puller when Berta stirred from her slumber and decided to participate in the event. Little by little, things began happening and the feet with rubbery hooves, followed by the pink nose and wet floppy ears appeared. We, Berta and I that is, rested a bit and then settled back in to our task. I thought if I could just pull a little harder the calf should come out so I put my right foot against Berta's rump, closed my eyes, and gritted my teeth. Berta got with the program in earnest and strained with simultaneous bellows just like the ladies in the delivery room in the soap opera Doctor's Hospital.

I opened my eyes to assess progress only to see that Berta had her tail straight up in the air and was delivering more than just the calf. I managed to close my eyes and mouth just in time to feel the hot, moist. fetid, green geyser hit me like a blast from a fire hose. Just then the calf came out too and I fell on my butt with the newborn slimy calf planted on my chest. Too stunned to do anything I sat there contemplating my manure filled navel. I heard an unidentifiable sound from behind that was a cross between a guffaw, a wheeze, a snort, a hiccup and a passing of gas. My befuddled mind finally realized that it was Pete who had come out to check on me just in time to see the whole rodeo. My hair, ears, eye sockets, and nostrils were full. It was down the back of my neck, all over my bare chest and was slowly trickling down inside my tightly whities. Even my rubber boots were full. Pete led me like the blind man that I was into the milking parlor and, adding insult to injury, sprayed me down with the hose used for washing cow udders. Pete said, "I didn't know whether to laugh or cry. By the way, mother and daughter are doing fine."

I had spare coveralls in the truck, so I stripped all the way down to nothing, hoping Mrs. Beck wouldn't put in a surprise appearance, hosed off, got into the clean coveralls and drove home for a shower and a well-deserved cold Molson beer. I swear I could hear Pete laughing all the way as I drove out the farm lane. I went back to the office to finish up appointments trying to defer the questions from the staff. The smirks and giggles indicated that Pete had already alerted them as to what had happened.

About an hour later the phone rang. It was Pete. "Hey, Doc. You better get your fanny back out here and finish the job. There are two more feet showing." I had forgotten to check the oven and see if there were any more goodies left inside. Berta had twin heifers. I carefully checked to be sure that there wasn't an unlikely third calf. I told Pete that I would add my dry-cleaning bill to his invoice. The *green* jokes were all too frequent at the office for the next few days: Green around the gills. Paid in greenbacks. See the world through green colored glasses. Is your hair growing faster? Does your dog like Greenies? Can't you hear? Got manure in your ears? Are you shit faced? After 30 years I can finally laugh about it, a little.

# WHAT'S FOR DINNER

We stood silently, waiting for the heavy cloud of dust to settle as we watched the green government stock truck rattle down into the valley below. The rumbling and backfiring of the exhaust echoed from the surrounding hills. Quiet finally settled in. We had been dropped off with our pack horses and a pile of gear at the end of a Forest Service road high up on Taneum ridge among the Douglas firs and Ponderosa pines of the Cascade Mountains. It was our job as trail crew to clear and maintain trails in the Wenatchee National Forest. My three crew members couldn't pack horses or cook, so as foreman I had my hands pretty full. We had renamed our three pack horses: Toolie, because he carried the chainsaw and tools, Kitchen, so named for obvious reasons, and House, because he carried the tent, sleeping bags, and personal gear. Especially important on this trip were extra chainsaw gas, as much pre-frozen food as possible, and extra water. The saw gas was needed because it had been an especially hard winter and the trail passed through lodge pole pine thickets which were especially prone to blowdown. Since we would be out for 10 days we pre-froze as much food as possible and buried it in the bottom of Kitchen's pack box in the horse grain to insulate it from thawing. We carried as much drinking water as possible because much of the trail followed the dry ridge tops and we had to descend into side canyons to replenish our supply and water the horses. We usually drank from streams and springs but the water quality and availability on this trip was a little sketchy.

Our responsibilities included improving the trail tread and kicking out as much loose rock as possible. We used the chainsaw to clear the trail of downed logs, and used a 12-foot pruning saw to cut low hanging branches that might slap a horseman in the face. We also worked on washouts, slides, mud holes, and minor detours as time allowed. At the end of each day we made a new camp but as chief wrangler and cook I had to prepare the meals and lunches for the following day and also tend to the pack horses. My crew members put the camp together and got a fire going but I had to start early and quit late to assure the horses got as much grazing time as possible.

On my day off I did the grocery shopping for our next week in the woods. There might have been a special on chuck steak or whole chicken at 19¢ a pound so we could look forward to a midweek baked potato and steak or fried chicken dinner. By the end of each day we were starved and we started our dinner meal with Fred's *specialty salad* of greens, vegetables, fruits, and meats. The greens were lettuce, spinach, and celery; vegetables included grated carrots, tomatoes, peas, and maybe beans; fruits usually involved grapes, raisons, apples, bananas, and oranges; and meats could be canned tuna, chipped beef, or precooked chicken. We filled a mixing bowl with this *conglomeration*, piled on a huge glob of *Tang* salad dressing, and each ate a large plateful as an appetizer before the main course. Main course meat was Monday: hamburger. Tuesday: fried whole chicken, Wednesday: chuck steak, Thursday: pre-baked turkey casserole, Friday: beans and wieners. After that the chef only needed a can opener. Throw in potatoes, a vegetable, and a whole package of Oreo cookies for desert and we were often still hungry. Liquid refreshment was usually a gallon or two of instant lemonade.

By the time I had the pack horses lined out on that hot August Monday morning, I was drenched in sweat. It ran down my face from beneath my hard hat, dripped off the end of my nose, and trickled down the small of my back. We groaned, gloved up, grabbed our tools, and headed up the trail into the ridge tops. There was a certain rhythm to our work which had evolved through the summer into reasonable efficiency and minimal conversation. Easy bantering talk was saved for rest breaks, lunch time, and around the evening campfire. Days one and two had passed uneventfully under a cloudless sky and hot sun with hawks and turkey vultures circling ominously overhead. Nights were always refreshingly chilly and warm sleeping bags were welcome as we snuggled in while listening to the coyote's serenade and owls hootenanny. By day five we were tired, dirty, and more than a little owly. We had had only enough water to drink and cook so our faces were streaked with muddy sweat and our bodies were, well, *unfragrant.* We hadn't even bothered to change into clean clothes. We were almost out of chainsaw gas and the pruning saw was getting dull. Someone had left the file at the last camp so we couldn't even sharpen our axes. As the day ended we took the stock down off the ridge to a little seep where we were able to get them enough muddy drinking water and then proceeded on up to our night's campsite. It was an old hunting camp called Camp Noble at a place called Peaches Ridge. Locals knew that it was really Camp No Bull because of the lack of success of a hunting party during elk season.

I got the pack saddles off the horses, brushed them, hobbled them, and sent them out to graze on the sparse ridge line grass while my crew mates put the camp together. I busied myself getting a dinner meal together for four very hungry mountain men. We were starved and were getting down to the last of our reasonably fresh food. I wrapped some potatoes in tin foil and tucked them in around the edge of the fire we had built in the camp's old fire pit. Then I threw an old oven rack on the fire so we could grill our chuck steak. We sat back almost drooling as we watched our dinner cook. It seemed like it took forever.

Then the fire exploded! And again, and again, and again! Not knowing what was happening we literally dove for cover behind logs and trees. Ashes, flaming bits of firewood, and projectiles were flying all around us. Even the pack horses galloped off to the safety of the tree line at the end of the clearing. Things finally quieted a little bit and someone said. "Does anyone have a change of shorts?" I cautiously ventured forward to see a smoking rifle cartridge in the pine needles at my feet. Then the fire exploded once more. So we sat and waited some more. Some prankster had buried 30-06 rifle cartridges down in the ashes of the old fire pit. When the fire got hot enough they started exploding. I don't think they would have hurt us but we certainly weren't laughing or taking any chances when the fireworks were going off.

But we were still starved and our hunger overcame our common sense so, hiding behind a tree, I used the 12-foot pruning saw to flip the grill, potatoes, and steak to safety outside of the firing range. At a safe distance away, we built another fire, dusted off the potatoes and meat, and finished cooking. Never has a charcoal broiled steak with totally natural organic grit seasoning tasted quite so good. I think we all slept lightly that night wondering if the fireworks were going to begin again. I won't elaborate the descriptive terms that came to mind as we contemplated the individuals who perpetrated this prank.

Following our usual routine, I got up at daylight the next morning to get the horses back out grazing. I put the cast iron frying pan on the new fire and cooked a pound of bacon, the left-over potatoes, a dozen eggs, and 48 hot cakes. After this morning snack our work day began. Not having a dog along to lick the dishes, we just wiped them down with paper towels and stowed them back in the kitchen pack box. The frying pan never got washed anyway. You didn't want to scrub away the seasoning and after all, it would get sterilized the next time you threw it on the fire. We put feed bags on the horses while we broke camp and were usually on the trail and working by 8 a. m.

By our final day of work, we had looped back to the original trail head where the head wrangler waited with the green truck. When we got back to the US Forest Service compound late that afternoon we told a dubious district Head Ranger about our adventure. He smiled and said, "I'm going to have to have you fellows arrested and fined for setting off fireworks in the National Forest."

# SONNY

I guess we had a fairly traditional childhood. My sister and I knew we were loved, but typically decisions were made by our parents with little input from us. Money was a little bit tight so we had to be content with what was allocated. Our parents had to negotiate the difficult balance between what their children wanted, what their children needed, and what was affordable. Consequently, there were only a few presents under the tree that had strictly entertainment value. Almost everything had some utilitarian purpose like *good clothes* for school. There was one flaw or inconsistency in the family plan for financial discipline, and it centered around my mother's love of and need for a horse. My poor father was trapped in the middle between my mother and her horse. The family eventually bought 5 acres with an unfinished house. My father was a college chemistry professor but now all his free time was consumed building a small horse barn, finishing the house, irrigating the pasture, and putting up a hay crop. He was wise enough to teach me to be a carpenter's assistant and do the farming but to also accept and appreciate the responsibility he placed on me. It's hard to get in trouble if you're kept busy enough.

Did you ever get a present you really didn't want? Well, that was perhaps the case here. One Friday afternoon in the spring when I was 10 years old I got off yellow bus #12 and ran into the house. We didn't know about TGIF back then but I'm sure that's what was going through my mind. Mother said, "Your horse is out in the corral." I can only imagine the expression that appeared on my face. I had absolutely no desire or expectation of getting a horse and my first thoughts centered on wondering how it might impact my seemingly endless list of chores and further limit my *fun* time. Mother and my sister each had a horse while I had a well-trained Schwinn bicycle. A bicycle was an ideal pet for me because it did not need to be fed, trained, or cared for. A horse certainly had not been an item for discussion around the dinner table. Mother explained that her cousin Katherine had gotten married and was moving to a distant city where there was no room for her horse. Mother said, "I know that his name is Sundown but I haven't even seen him yet myself. Let's go out and get acquainted."

Sonny, as we came to call him, was waiting for us in the shade of the loafing shed of our small horse barn. He gave us a friendly nicker as we approached. When I got close enough he licked my hand and sniffed my face. It was a classic equine "Hello." There was a black saddle and a black bridle with funny looking braided leather English reins the like of which I had never seen before. Mother knew he was coming and had been told a little bit about him but her cousin just dropped him off, left the saddle and bridle on the top fence rail, and drove away back home to Spokane. There were no notes, no messages, no batteries, and no owner's instruction or maintenance manual to read.

He was a rich shiny black with perfect white star the middle of his forehead. His mane was full and long and his tail touched the ground. What are soft eyes? I don't know if a definition really exists but he had them. Many *black* horses brown out as the strong summer sun bleaches their hair coat but Sonny was a real jet black. He was just shy of 16 hands and his long slender legs belied his American Saddlebred bloodlines.

We found an old green wool blanket with *US Army* stenciled in the corner that the moths hadn't devoured. By folding it many times we created a make do saddle blanket. We put on the saddle and bridle and after mother gave me a boost up we soon discovered that we couldn't make the stirrups short enough to fit me. I tried to turn him by neck reining but I might have been speaking a foreign language. Mother said, "It looks like he only knows how to direct rein." I tried to kick him into a trot but he just shifted into a fast but strangely smooth collected gait. I had no idea what he was doing but it was fast and smooth and sure fun to ride.

Mother talked with her uncle, Katherine's father, that evening on the telephone. In those days, such conversations were short because long-distance calls were deemed to be expensive. He said, "Didn't Katherine tell you that Sundown was five gaited?" We subsequently learned what five-gaited meant. Sundown could walk, trot, and canter but he also had a slow gait and rack. The slow gait and rack have a four-beat rhythm where there's always one foot bearing weight on the ground. Consequently, the ride is smooth and you don't get bounced up and down as you do in a trot.

Thus, began our training process. He trained me to love horses and appreciate the versatility of our equine friends and I taught him how to neck rein, play western horse games, and travel on mountain trails. My sister belonged to a horse club which was primarily dedicated to horse games where you competed against other clubs at playdays or gymkhanas. So, I joined too.

But first we had to learn how to communicate with each other. I didn't know anything about training him to neck rein but I realized that if I rode him towards a wall he was going to want me to tell him which way to turn. That, with also gently whacking him on the side of the neck with a piece of rubber hose, seemed to get the job done. His intelligence, enthusiasm, and willingness to please made me feel like a real horse trainer. I think he was actually doing most of the training.

Mother and my sister liked to go trail riding and now that we had three horses I *had* to go along with them. My father knew nothing about horses and therefore he got a free pass. Later that summer I realized that I actually really enjoyed these rides. We had no horse trailer so we had to ride the county roads to get to the foothills. Sonny was not afraid of water or logs and actually preferred to jump them. Thus, he trained me in survival jumping. He was also always on the lookout for scary bushes, suspicious stumps, sasquatches, potential floods or landslides, and strange or suspicious noises. Because of his protective caution, we usually managed to survive all these extremely dangerous trail hazards and I often managed to stay in the saddle.

The riding club competed in equine games like pole bending, barrels (a four barrel clover leaf pattern in those days), musical sacks, egg races, water bucket brigades, and other relays. Sonny loved it. Show a chalk line, a starter pistol pointed in the air, or a sailing cowboy hat to Sonny and he was a totally different beast. Every weekend during the summer there was a playday somewhere in another community. Somebody's dad always had a cattle truck (there were very few horse trailers in those days) and on Sundays the club drove off for a day of family horse games. Few of us even had TV. Cell phones were only imagined in Dick Tracy Sunday comics. Families talked to each other, played together, and even sat down and had meals together. It was good stuff!

Pole bending was Sonny's favorite event and thus it was mine. He wasn't extremely fast but his great coordination made up for his lack of speed. The event involved weaving down and back through a row of 6 poles kind of like what we now see in canine agility trials. During the summers when I was 11, 12, and 13 we were rarely defeated in this event.

Another event was called the Walk, Trot, and Scoot. One horse walked to the end of the arena, a second horse trotted back, and the third horse made a round trip at a full gallop. My sister's horse could walk impressively fast but Sonny could rack. There were no horses that could trot as fast as he could rack and nobody realized that he was doing a totally different gait. We could have used a slow pony for the final galloping stage because we already had such a large lead. I don't think anyone ever beat us in this event.

Some summer weekends were spent horse camping. With bulging saddle bags, a sleeping bag tied on top, and Army ponchos we rode into the mountains to spend the weekend riding trails and cooking over a campfire. Sonny was happiest when right in camp. He loved to get his share of morning hotcakes and seem to enjoy an occasional bite of ham sandwich as long as the mustard wasn't spread too thick. During the day time we could turn him loose with hobbles in the mountain meadows to graze. At night, of course, we kept him tied close to camp and I usually placed my sleeping bag nearby but just out of stomping range.

We also learned that's Sonny had been trained to drive and could pull a buggy. An old lady in our rural neighborhood had a tired old buggy in her barn and she happily granted permission to clean it up, paint it, and make it functional again. With some old borrowed light harness, a box of brass rivets, and a hand leather stitching awl, we were in the equine carriage business. He transported my sister and her boyfriend to school on the last day of their senior year one spring. He proudly pulled the buggy for a pretty small-town rodeo queen for the local Rodeo Parade with me as her cowboy coachman.

Time passes and little boys turn into bigger boys. Schoolwork, athletics, and summer jobs begun to put a major damper on my horse time. We still found time for occasional game days and camping trips but they were a less frequent occurrence.

When I turned 18, I got a job as foreman of the USFS trail maintenance crew for our local USFS Ranger District. Sonny was still part of the family but at the age of 23 he had been relegated to semi-retirement. One hot Friday afternoon I got home from ten days in the woods doing trail work. I showered, changed into clean clothes, and went out to the barn to check on Sonny and the rest of the horses. There was a scrawled note in pencil on a nail over the tack room door. It only said, "I came to pick up Sundown." That was all. I had to sit down on a nearby bale of hay to contemplate my loss. I had to realize that I had never really owned Sonny but over those nine years strong bonds had been established.

I looked into the tack room to see that the original saddle, an almost brand-new bridle, a fairly expensive horse pad, a halter, a brush, and even a curry comb were also gone. I had to admit it was a small price to pay for the years I had with a wonderful horse that was *never really mine.* We later learned that Katherine now had a daughter old enough to ride. Sonny proved to be a capable babysitter and as the little girl's skills grew, he became her first show horse. I hope this little girl grew to love and appreciate what a fine horse she had and could *call her own.*

There have been twelve horses over almost 65 years that have enriched my life since Sonny but when I think back and make a mental list of the names, Sonny is always at the top. When the computer log-in asks for an additional security word, you might be able to imagine what I choose.

**Brownie**

# THE NIGHT VISITOR

Mrs. Holly came in with a wistful smile on her face struggling to maintain her usual upbeat cheerful attitude. Her gray hair was in a long braid down her back secured at the end with some Indian beadwork. I don't think she ever had it cut. She wore clean but well-worn Levi's and still had the firm trim figure of a hard-working rancher's wife. She was accompanied by her two adult daughters, Jill and Mary, who were carrying the family's old white miniature poodle Misty. Misty was usually amazingly clean and white considering that she helped with the cattle ranch chores. Today, however, the dog was bedraggled and lying quietly in the girl's arms. We had scheduled them for the last appointment of the day realizing that tough decisions might have to be made. Misty had been having mild seizures for several years but they had now become intractable and unresponsive to any medications. Not long after recovering from one seizure another one set in and the poor little dog was exhausted and bewildered. The Holly's were a practical ranch family and knew there was only one decision that could be made. There were no tears in anyone's eyes but a sad look of resolve was on everyone's face. Pushing her bifocals up on her nose and instinctively reaching back for her braid, Mrs. Holly took a deep breath and said, "The girls and I have come to the conclusion that the time has come and we are ready to put Misty down. Can you do this for us?"

Complicating matters, however, was the fact that her husband, Tom, was in the hospital recovering from lung cancer surgery. He had been looking like a refugee from an African famine and had been extremely frustrated by his inability to hold up his end of the ranching responsibilities. "How is your husband doing?" I enquired.

"Not well. Misty is his favorite. The Blue Heelers are more like farm equipment but Misty was his buddy. She followed him everywhere on the ranch, barked at the cows, and helped drive the quad. He's worried sick about her."

We did what we had to do. "We have a hole dug under the weeping willow in the back yard where Misty can look out over the corrals and pasture," Jill said.

I phoned the ranch a few days later to inquire after Tom. "He understood that we had no choice with Misty but he is just lying there in his hospital bed staring at the ceiling. He really doesn't want visitors and I feel like he has given up and doesn't care anymore," said Mrs. Holly.

I paused and then asked, "Can you and the girls come in this afternoon? I have a suggestion I would like to make." We had a client who bred miniature poodles who was moving back East to an apartment and needed to place puppies from her last litter. One six-week-old brown female puppy was my favorite and I had asked her if she would bring the puppy in. "I think I have a home for her." I said.

When the Hollys were seated on the exam room bench I brought the puppy in. Three faces lit up like Christmas trees. They immediately guessed my plan but Mary asked, "Can we take the puppy into the hospital?"

"I don't know but I think we need to try," I said. We vaccinated, dewormed, loved the puppy, and spent a half hour sitting on the floor playing and getting acquainted.

"She's perfect," said Mrs. Holly. "How much is she?"

I smiled with my answer. "She's free to a home approved by me and I approve."

I didn't learn the outcome of my experiment for 6 weeks when the Hollys, all five of them, came in for the puppy's (Brownie) next vaccinations. Tom looked pretty puny but the old sparkle was back in his eyes. Mrs. Holly told the story.

"I put the puppy in the front pocket of my Carhartts and we just walked past the front reception desk right into the hospital. The receptionist and nurses were used to seeing us and we tried to look innocent. I felt like a criminal. Tom was just lying there staring into space. I put the puppy on the foot of the bed and stepped back to see what would happen. Brownie looked around, walked up to the head of the bed, wagged her fuzzy tail, and gave Tom a big ol' lick right on the kisser. Tom looked down, startled, and a smile slowly spread over his face. It was the first smile we had seen in months. The girls and I were almost giddy until a nurse burst through the door with Tom's next round of medicine. She looked at the scene and started to say something. She reconsidered and backed out of the room without saying a word. A few minutes later head nurse Ratched charged through the door. We all held our breath. She smiled serenely and said, 'I see that your granddaughter has come in to visit you Tom. What a treat! Just try not to let her disturb the rest of the patients.' Over the next hour, I think the entire nursing staff came in to meet Tom's *granddaughter* Brownie."

Someone said, "That's sure a funny name for a beautiful little girl."

"We stayed well past visiting hours but nobody complained," said Mrs. Holly

Tom was able to go back to ranching at half speed faithfully accompanied by his side kick Brownie. The girls married and Brownie eventually even had cousins to play with. Tom made it almost to eighty and Brownie passed in her sleep one night a year or so later when almost 18 years old. Brownie is resting quietly alongside Misty.

# HEY DOC, CAN YOU CUT MY HORSE

I hadn't been a *vet* for very long, but I knew I had <u>all</u> the answers and could handle <u>any</u> animal medical problem. I had a drawer full of shiny stainless steel surgical instruments, a stethoscope draped around my neck, and a new set of blue coveralls. It was great to be young and to *know it all.* Early one Friday morning, Judy, my receptionist, said, "Doctor, there's a Mr. Drake on the phone for you." I finished castrating and treating the abscess on the former tomcat I was working on, scrubbed up, and picked up the phone.

Mr. Drake explained, "I'm an airline captain and only home on weekends. I have a 12-year-old Thoroughbred stallion that's kind of rank and I need to have him cut. He needs a personality adjustment. Can you do that?" This was exactly the kind of challenge a young male veterinarian with excess testosterone couldn't resist, so I eagerly set it up for the next morning.

It was a cool, crisp morning with a light breeze; the kind of day when you lunge your horse for 20 minutes before you climb on. Even the Rhode Island Red rooster on the barn weather vane seemed pretty cocky. The vinyl fences were white, the driveway was paved, and the barn still smelled like rubber stall mats and new cedar lumber. I was a little embarrassed to be working out of the trunk of a sedan instead of a big pickup with a big fiberglass vet box on the back. However, I expected that would all come about in due time. Mr. Drake met me out front in his new white Stetson, snap button Wrangler shirt, and alligator Tony Lama boots but you knew he was mostly hat and not too much cowboy. He said, "I got him for a steal at the auction three weeks ago and they delivered him but I haven't been able to touch him since." I tried, unsuccessfully, to ignore the fire alarm bells ringing in the back of my head but forged on ahead anyway. We entered the barn and moseyed over to the stall. The horse was spectacular.

Shiny black, almost 17 hands tall, beautifully muscled with nostrils flared and ears plastered back flat against his head. He dared us to get within biting or striking range. He was one of the biggest Thoroughbreds I had ever seen. Trying to look bigger and tougher than I really was, I managed to get a halter on him and with a stud chain in place we led him out to a clean piece of grass for his *taking out* party.

With his jaw clenched and his eyes squinted almost shut Mr. Drake managed to hold on while I got a good dose of tranquilizer into the horse's jugular vein. Trying to look confident, I waited for the drug to take effect. And waited, and waited, and waited. Nothing happened. He just stood there looking more dangerous and challenging us to get anywhere within range. I got lucky and managed to get another dose and a half in. Moving targets might work with a shotgun but needles are another story. I had never put so much tranquilizer into a horse. He finally hung his head and relaxed with a blissful expression so I loaded my syringe with the real stuff: the general anesthetic. He seemed to know what I had in mind for he was suddenly wide awake again and was watching my every move. I snubbed him to a post and got the drug in before he could pull the barn down on top of us.

As soon as he hit the ground I was prepared to work fast, but I wasn't fast enough. Before I could get him trussed up he staggered back to his feet and glared stupidly but menacingly back at us. I should have gotten back in my car and driven away but pride and testosterone ruled again. I managed to get another full dose of anesthetic in and he finally collapsed in an explosive heap on the ground. It made me fully appreciate bomb squad personnel. I tied a back leg out of the way, scrubbed him and cut away with a vengeance and with an evil grin on my face. It's amazing how time flies and how fast you can work when you fear for your life. Finishing up with anti-inflammatories, antibiotics and vaccinations, I wiped the sweat off my forehead with blood still dripping off my fingers, removed the rope and walked to my car to wash up and put my surgical instruments away. I looked up to check on the horse only to see that he was already on his feet looking meaner and more threatening than ever. It's hard to push a horse away with the end of a limp halter rope but Mr. Drake was certainly trying. We got the former stallion into a corral and turned him loose with the halter still on and the lead rope dragging in the dirt.

We stood outside the corral with our boots placed picturesquely on the bottom rail of the fence for a few minutes catching our wind and collecting our thoughts. Mr. Drake got a peculiar look on his face and said, "I'm sure glad that's over. You're the fourth vet to try. One never even got out of his truck."

I stood there dumbfounded and then said a few things I shouldn't have but said them anyway. "Why didn't you tell me?"

"I was afraid you would turn me down," Mr. Drake said. "My wife told me that we either had to cut him, or shoot him, or we'd be getting a divorce." After a lot of time and money spent on training and sweaty blankets, that former Tennessee Stud turned into a pretty good 3-day event horse.

That early generation of tranquilizer and anesthetic drugs was notorious for unpredictable results, especially in hot excited horses. Thoroughbreds could do irreparable damage to themselves even while in the process of recovering from a surgery such as the famous race horse Ruffian. Their fright and flight switch seems to stay turned on. Newer drugs are much smoother and a horse may start grazing even before he tries to get up. Being older and wiser now, and given another chance, I, too, might just stay in my truck and just keep on driving.

**"Something seems to be missing. I can't figure out just what."**

# A LONG WALK HOME

I was the young foreman of a USFS trail crew and it was our job to build and maintain mountain trail in the Cle Elum District of Wenatchee National Forest. It was a great summer job for a teenage college student trying to earn his next year's tuition. The restlessness and cobwebs accumulated in nine months of 5 hours a day classroom time were quickly forgotten in the mountain air. Hard work, clean air, cold water, no desks, and relative independence made for a growing experience. Actually, I wore many hats due to the relative inexperience of the rest of my crew. They didn't know the area, couldn't cook, and knew nothing about horses. Consequently, I was also guide, provisioner, cook, and wrangler. Time flies when you are busy from dawn to dusk. I had to wrangle the horses, plan and cook the meals, organize and supervise the day's work, and occasionally smooth ruffled feathers of my sometimes-grumpy crew. At least I didn't feel guilty when avoiding the least favorite of our tasks: manning the 12-foot pruning saw to cut off low hanging branches that could slap a horseman in the face. We were working the Middle Fork Trail of the Teanaway River and were in its headwaters above Paris Creek about 12 miles from the trail head. It was a steep narrow mountain valley that ran from the lush lowland meadows filled with cottonwoods and their summer snowstorm fuzz to the rocky reaches of stunted high elevation alpine firs. The weather had been clear and warm but cool and crisp at night. We wore short sleeves in the daytime but snuggled in warm sleeping bags at night. We usually moved camp every day after working 3 to 5 miles of trail. You had to know the country to plan camps where there was grass for the horses and water and wood for the camp.

A full bladder and the stomping feet of impatient stock made a morning alarm clock unnecessary. I unzipped my bag, shucked my long underwear, pulled on my pants, opened the tent fly, and stepped into the morning mist. It was 5 a.m. and getting light. I had to get up, kick the fire together, and get the pack horses out in the meadow to graze. We broke camp while I put together a light breakfast- usually hot cereal with canned milk, 12 - 16 hotcakes each, 4 slices of bacon, 3 eggs, 2 pieces of toast piled with preserves, and hot coffee or cocoa. By 8 a.m. the horses were packed, lunches made and packed, and we were working our way down the trail trimming low handing branches, cutting out down timber, clearing rocks, and cutting small trees that encroached on the trail right of way.

Chief, the lead horse, was a huge bossy buckskin draft cross who carried the tools, gas, oil, and chain saw and could be usually counted to ground tie when the chainsaw came out to snarl its way through a log. Chum, a smaller buckskin, was a pigeon toed stumbler who carried the unbreakable camp items like tent, stove, personal gear, clothes, and sleeping bags. He was well mannered and quiet and did his job willingly without complaint. Avalanche, a friendly soft coated large mostly white paint, was the grocery store and could be counted on to bring up the rear and carry the eggs along to the next campsite without breakage. Norm, Mike, and Ted made up the rest of the two-legged crew, and being older than I, made my job as foreman a little more interesting and required more diplomacy than bossiness.

In the 12 miles of this trail there must have been 20 creek/river crossings. Each ford required a decision whether to rock hop across and risk falling in or to pull off boots and wade barefooted. We usually waited until later in the summer to work this trail because the river would be too fast and deep early in the spring to ford so many times. We agreed with this late season timing because this was prime huckleberry country and they were a great addition to our morning hotcakes and evening muffins.

I had worked on ahead leaving the rest of the crew to lead the pack horses along. If I came to a down log I would wait for the crew with the chain saw to arrive to cut it out. I was working with a small double bitted axe chopping out small trees. You would bend them over with your boot and chop them off near the ground with the axe, being careful to avoid toes. I wonder how many thousand Christmas trees I murdered during those summers. The trail passed through sunny morning meadows into mountain shadow and between the massive boulders of an ancient rock fall. Car and bus sized chunks of sandstone mountain filled the valley floor as the trail dodged between them on its meandering way downstream. I stopped to wipe the sweat off my forehead and suddenly felt a slight chill. The hair on the back of my neck prickled like the hackles on a dog's back but I couldn't see or hear anything amiss. I felt like I was being watched but attributed it to a slight up-valley morning breeze. Picking up my axe I worked my way on down the trail looking forward to our mid-morning rest break. As 10 a.m. approached, I stopped near a stream crossing to await the rest of the crew.

And then I got that prickly feeling again. After a few seconds, I sensed a hollow drumming vibration in the ground and then heard the ring of steel shod hooves on the rocks of the rough trail. Looking up the trail I saw my shop, home, and kitchen coming down the trail at a full trot. I dropped my axe, picked up a green branch and with my hard hat in the other hand stepped into the trail to flag down the oncoming freight train. But it didn’t stop or even blow its whistle. So, I dove back out of the trail into the prickly brushes to avoid becoming mountain road kill as my unstoppable pack string headed down the valley to parts unknown. Dusting the dirt off the seat of my pants and wiping the dirt off my face I waited for the rest of my crew to arrive. They explained that as they passed through the rock maze

Momma Bear and Baby Bear suddenly appeared in the middle of the trail. I can imagine the Bear family with purple stained lips and my crew with perhaps brown stained shorts scattering in opposite directions. The horses had seen many bears and I suspect rather than being frightened they just took advantage of the opportunity to head for home. My crew still had their hand tools so I told them (probably suggested) to keep working as best they could and I would go after the horses. I assumed they would stop to eat in the next good meadow and I would be back in time for lunch. How terribly wrong I would prove to be.

Tying my sweat shirt around my waist I headed down the trail at a jog. I was in good shape but running in Vibram soled work boots is a little harder. I soon came to a creek crossing and noticed that the water droplets scattered by the horses as they splashed through the stream were still expanding. They couldn't be far ahead of me and I sometimes wondered if I heard them. I redoubled my effort hoping to overtake them but after a mile or so realized that they weren't going to stop. After lacing my boots tighter, I settled into a mile eating jog determined to reclaim my lost property. I ran and I ran and I ran. I lost count of the creek and river crossings, each recently traversed by the horses.

Midday turned into afternoon and afternoon turned into evening and evening turned into dusk. The trail head and parking lot came and went and I soon was jogging down the county road. I reached the first/last residence on the county road and looking far ahead around a curve saw my horses still making good time. Using my last bit of energy, I ducked through the fence, ran across a horse pasture and just managed to reach the county road stop sign before the horses did. They stopped and waited for me and Chief yawned as if to say, "What are you looking at? You have some sort of a problem?"

But what had I caught up to? Chief's Decker pack saddle was upside down and all the gear gone. Chum was missing two shoes, a pack saddle, and was lame. Avalanche was pretty much OK but had cinch galls on his girth. The owners were home so I got permission to leave Chum there in the pasture for later pickup. I had no difficulty accepting their offer for a quick hot meal and some snacks for the trail. After readjusting the saddle rigging on Chief and Avalanche, I headed back up the trail. The horses were also tired so we did a double walk and ride: ride one, ride two, and then walk one. Sitting on a pack saddle is pretty uncomfortable but it was better than walking at that time.

By then it was 10 p.m. and pitch dark. The sky was overcast and there was no moon. It was dark, dark, dark. When riding I often got slapped in the face by low hanging branches that I couldn't see in the blackness. (This is why we carried a pruning saw.) I had left caches of gear in the middle of the trail and amazingly Chief stopped at each of the piles. It was so dark I couldn't see them. You get to know your horses pretty well if you repack them by braille in total darkness. Eventually we had recovered most of the gear but I no longer had a horse to ride. So, it was back to shank's mare but it was so dark I couldn't find the trail.

Chief seemed resigned to travel back up the valley so I walked behind him holding onto his tail for propulsion and guidance. He was polite enough not to lift it for me except for occasional polite little toots. Fortunately, the bears and other dangerous zoo animals were asleep in bed, for it would have been difficult to do hand to hand combat in total darkness. I had seen Kung Fu movies so I was ready for them nevertheless. The occasional "Hoot! Hoot!" of spotted owls was more reassuring than frightening. Grazing animals and small mammals were still about and I could hear the snap of branches and rustling bushes as they scattered in front of us. At least I could ride across the river crossings on top of the pack boxes and the horses had their waterproof boots on.

About an hour before dawn I struggled up a steep pitch and smelled wood smoke. Then I saw a welcome camp fire in the distance. My crew had located some of the gear, made camp, built a big fire, and were sleeping on the ground around it. I had traveled over 30 miles, much of it in total darkness, to bring the horses back to camp. Norm woke, yawned, stretched, and said, "What took you so long?"

# EYE SEE YOU

Washoe was the first chimpanzee (and non-human primate) to learn American Sign Language (ASL). She eventually acquired a vocabulary of 350 to 400 signs. In so doing, she totally redirected our comprehension and research regarding animal learning, communication, and tool using. She was born in West Africa in 1965 and was acquired by the Air Force for potential Space Program research. Dr. Alan Gardner and Dr. Roger Fouts raised Washoe (named after Washoe County, Arizona) from infancy in a human household environment and taught her ASL in the process. After the research faze of Washoe's life was completed, Dr. Fouts was unwilling to just abandon her so when he relocated to Central Washington University in 1980, Washoe and her extended adopted family were brought along to hopefully spend the rest of their life in a sanctuary environment.

Dr. Fouts' daughter and my son were in the same first grade class and the two families subsequently became acquainted.

Eventually I became the veterinary care provider for Washoe and her four housemates. Fortunately, there was little need for my services. The chimpanzees did have occasional family squabbles with minor wounds and bites and did require occasional blood work and checks for parasites. Unfortunately, since chimpanzees are at least twice as strong as humans, a brief general anesthetic is required to properly examine them. Obviously, we avoided this if at all possible. It was educational collaborating with my personal family physician if I was troubled with some diagnosis. I think he was amazed at the similarity between human medical conditions and that of our nearest primate relatives. We did make occasional 2 a.m. visits to our local hospital carrying an anesthetized chimpanzee into the imaging department.

Initially, I was just a friendly occasional visitor in Washoe's home environment. I typically wore a western-type pull on boot and it appeared Washoe had never seen this type of footwear before. She had a shoe fetish and like the Philippines first lady Imelda Marcos, had a private collection of them amongst her most prized possessions. When we were still on good *speaking* terms, Washoe recognized me by signing shoe. As time went on she had other less flattering signs with which to identify me because she knew I might be inflicting pain. She might have thought better of me if I had shown up wearing a yellow hat. Did she have a copy of *Curious George* in her library?

At that time, the five chimpanzees living quarters were in one of the labs of the CWU psychology department. These facilities required daily cleaning which was accomplished with a high-pressure water spraying system. On one occasion, there was a splash back of spray directly back into Washoe's face. Obviously, she was startled but when she recovered she had one eye squinted tightly shut and was guarding it with her hand. We waited anxiously to see if she improved or would at least let us examine her eye. On multiple occasions, she would approach the enclosure fence but keep her eye closed and protected.

After 24 hours, we finally came to the reluctant conclusion that we needed to examine the eye to make sure it wasn't damaged or if some treatment was required. We discussed this in Washoe’s presence and came to the realization that we were going to have to anesthetize her to properly examine the eye. No doubt our words and body language communicated to Washoe all of our conflicted innermost thoughts. We retreated to a nearby room to whisper our plans and to prepare the anesthetic drugs and the blowgun to deliver them. I reluctantly entered her room one last time to see where she was and plan an approach. She was expecting me.

Traveling on hind feet and front knuckles as chimpanzees do, she bounded right over to the enclosure fence to greet us. It took a moment to realize what had changed. Her big brown almost human eyes were wide open. They were bright, clear, there was no discharge, and they seem to be expressing hope that we would not proceed with our plans. We had been played! She obviously had an uncanny ability to read and interpret our non-verbal body language and understand the gist of our spoken word. Did she just enjoy the attention or was she capable of making a joke? As we learn more about our non-human primate relatives I don't think anything will surprise me regarding their almost human characteristics and abilities. Chimpanzees thoroughly enjoy games of tickle and chase and perhaps this was just a variation. But she clearly understood that the game had gone too far and was about to backfire on her. It was time to come clean or accept the consequences.

Washoe died in 2007 at the amazing age of 42. Her obituary was published in the New York Times newspaper.

**RIP!**

**WASHOE**

# MOTHER'S LAST RIDE

When I was a baby, my mother developed the slow insidious form of multiple sclerosis. We were always given the mysterious explanation that she had had a *break down.* The disease was not medically diagnosed for 18 years, so she struggled physically through life not knowing what had been wrong all that time.. It took 18 years to discover what can now be learned with a 15-minute MRI. She taught English, Latin and Spanish in middle and high school, but by the end of each week she was worn out and weekends were often spent recovering only to begin again the following Monday. I was on my own for Saturday and Sunday breakfasts and lunches. It was a relief to her and the family when we finally had an answer as to what the problem had been.

I traveled to New England for university but in the meantime my mother met a coed attending our local college. Mother wrote (it seemed too expensive to call long distance) asking if it was

OK for Linda to ride my horse while I was away at school. I said, "Sure. As long as she knows what she's doing it should be a good thing." I didn't meet Linda until 2 years later during the summer after I received my BA.

Mother said one evening, "I invited Linda over for the weekend."

I said, "Oh? I suppose I'm expected to waste my weekend and keep her entertained?"

"No, but you might like to meet her." Well, Linda was supposed to stay for Saturday and Sunday, but she didn't leave until Wednesday morning. I guess *Mothers do know best.*

Linda and I dated long distance that winter but the following spring I got my draft notice. This was the peak of the Vietnam War and *The Army Wanted Me.* The attraction wasn't mutual. Mother suggested that the three of us go on a horse pack trip before I went off into the Army. I suggested that we do a 14 mile ride up into the North Fork of the Taneum where there was a trail shelter. We gathered tack, sleeping bags, warm clothes, food, and camp cookery and prepared for our adventure. It had been a mild winter but I was still concerned about snow remaining on the trail that far into the mountains during that early part of June.

My aunt delivered us and our three American Saddlebred horses to the trailhead with her horse truck because we only had a two-horse trailer. It was a struggle getting mother up into the saddle but she rode with a huge smile on her face once we got underway. Not having a pack horse, we had to attach everything to our saddles with horn bags and saddle bags with the bed rolls tied on top. Looking like mountain men on our heavily laden horses we left the warmth of the truck and started up the trail. The vegetation started with Ponderosa pine, then transitioned to fir, hemlock, and finally alpine fir as we climbed the trail that followed the creek. Steller's jays and Douglas squirrels squawked and complained and hawks made a screeching cry from above as we intruded into their territory. The icy foamy water at the fords was belly deep to the horses and we occasionally had to plunge through the deep snow drifts remaining on parts of the trail shaded by the deep timber.

After about 3 hours, mother said she was tired and needed a break. We found a clearing where we could get off, stretch our legs, loosen the cinches, and tie the horses. Mother's legs were so tired and weak she could hardly walk, so we got out the sleeping bags for her to lie down on. I got a good fire going for hot chocolate and soup. When we called mother to tell her that lunch was ready we discovered she was sound asleep. We let her sleep for an hour, ate our lunch and snacks, and then got back on the horses to continue our ride to the mountain camp. More fords, snowdrifts, and downed timber followed but we finally struggled in just at dusk. Mother collapsed onto the pile of sleeping bags but she had a smile of accomplishment on her face. There were the beginnings of spring grass peeking through in the meadow, so we hobbled the horses and turned them out. We got a roaring fire going and set up camp. The chuck steak broiled over the coals and potatoes wrapped in foil and buried alongside the fire were delicious. A whole package of gourmet Oreo cookies for desert never tasted so good. I gathered up the horses and tied them under the trees within the firelight. They got a small ration of grain in their nose bags and we secured their saddle blankets to their backs for added warmth. As the fire died down and the coals glowed in the dark, the hooting owls and calling coyotes serenaded us as we drifted off into sleep.

Warm morning sunshine woke us but there were threatening dark storm clouds off to the west. The smell of bacon and hot cakes to be washed down with hot chocolate got mother out of her sleeping bag. After breakfast Linda and I decided to ride up to a pass beneath the shoulder of a sandstone mountain leaving mother back at the shelter. She had a huge pile of wood we had dragged in to keep the fire going and a stack of pancakes to feed the friendly camp robbers. We climbed up the switch backs into the freshening wind which swirled away the horse's steaming breath. It had started snowing at the saddle of the ridge when we turned around to descend back to the camp. By the time we got there it was a full-blown blizzard with minimal visibility. The horses needed to feed but the storm drove them down wind away from camp, so I got on my horse bareback and pulled my poncho up over my head and dozed there warm and snug while the horses fed. A half hour later I startled awake to discover that our three horses were all part of a herd of 20 elk all grazing tail to the wind in the clearing.

We woke the next morning to 6 inches of new snow but with a clear sky and a warming sun that soon had the melting snow dripping off the trees. A snowshoe rabbit in his mottled spring coat and a mule deer doe with ribs showing above her pregnant belly loitered at the edge of the clearing. We hated to leave but *duty called* and we only brought enough food for three days. The horses instinctively found the trail through the snow and needed no encouragement traveling down valley to the trailhead.

Two days later when she delivered me to the bus out of town to go off to boot camp, mother, with tears in her eyes, thanked me for the wonderful ride and camping trip. "I suspect that it might have been my last ride." We lost her a few years later to lung cancer but felt blessed to have been able to share that time with her.

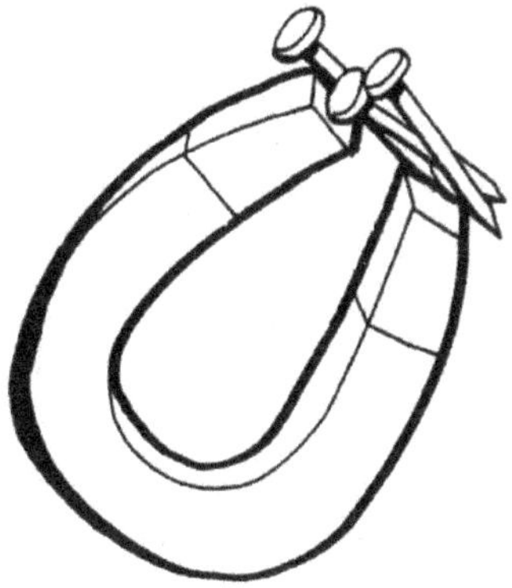

# GONE FISHIN'

I'm sure Bobby was beautiful in her owner's eyes. But can a bull terrier ever be called truly beautiful? Obviously, beauty is in the eye of the beholder. These are the party animals from the Spuds McKenzie Bud Light beer commercials of the 1980's. Bobby had an egg-shaped head, huge nose, little pig eyes, short ears, white hair coat, and the body of an NFL linebacker. Fortunately, Bull Terriers are sweet tempered loving family dogs and such was the case with Bobby. They in no way have the dangerous disposition potential of the other breed with a similar name: the Staffordshire Pitbull Terrier.

Bobby was a prize-winning show dog. She had a professional trainer/handler who traveled around North America taking her on the canine show circuit. If she placed well enough in the show ring, she would be retired for a career as a professional mother to produce valuable puppies for sale to potential pet owners.

When Bobby came in heat, Roberta, Bobby's owner, carefully sequestered her away so there was no possibility of an amorous encounter with the overly friendly neighbor's handsome mongrel male dog. One spring when Bobby was in season, she was, as usual, locked up in her crate with a soft snuggly blanket and a few of her favorite toys to keep her occupied. Males are only partially responsible for unintended breedings, for females' instinct drives them to also search for a partner. But being incarcerated only increased Bobby's anxiety and frustration. When put away, Bobby was proudly sporting her rhinestone bejeweled choke chain collar. (Bull Terriers are exceedingly strong and owners require a little advantage (the choke chain) in order to have some control over them from the other end of the leather leash.) A few hours later Roberta returned to check on Bobby only to discover that the beautiful choke chain collar was missing. Being uncertain whether one had been on in the first place, she replaced it with another. When Roberta came back a few hours later, it too was, in fact, missing. It was not hidden in the bedding and had not fallen out on the floor so it seemed there was only one possible place to which it could have disappeared: down Alice's Rabbit Hole. So, Bobby and I were presented with the opportunity to get more intimately reacquainted.

An X-ray confirmed our greatest fears. There were two choke chains grinning at us like Cheshire Cats from inside Bobby's stomach. We discussed the possibilities: a conservative wait and see approach to see if they might exit through the usual express channels, or surgery to remove the offending objects. Roberta said, "Bobby is my prize show dog. I would certainly prefer not to have a large surgical scar on her belly." So attempting the conservative approach first was an obvious no-brainer. However, two days of unhappy retching seem to indicate that this approach would not be successful.

"I have a harebrained idea", I said. "I think I'm going to go on a fishing adventure." Cattle sometimes accidentally consume sharp metallic objects such as wire or nails which can do serious damage under the influence of strong digestive tract peristalsis. One way to attempt prevention of damage is to put a large strong magnet (shaped like a small wiener) in their stomach (rumen) to collect these metallic objects. My plan was to jam one of these magnets into the end of a piece of radiator hose to see if I could attract the choke chains. We tested the magnet on another choke chain and there was strong attraction, so we anesthetized Bobby and easing a lubricated magnet containing rubber hose over her lips and through her gums and said, "Look out stomach, here it comes." So, through her throat and down her esophagus into her stomach and we commenced fishing. After wiggling the bait around enticingly, we carefully pulled the hose back out and we're delighted to see dangling from the end, a captured rhinestone encrusted choke chain collar. Several more fishing attempts resulted in tricking the second choke chain as well. After a little washing, scrubbing, and polishing the rhinestone choke chain was as beautiful as ever. About an hour later Bobby staggered out to the reception room and through the front door to be assisted into the back seat for the trip home. We modestly patted ourselves on the back at the success of our barnyard ingenuity. Fishing had been good that day. The choke chains were biting.

About two years later Roberta scheduled a routine appointment for Bobby. She said, "I have three things to show you." First, she showed me an article she had written and had published in her breed journal about Bobby's problem and its resolution. Second, she showed me a trophy for best of breed from the previous season's show circuit. Then she said, "Wait a minute and I will show you the third thing." She dashed out to her car and came back in carrying a laundry basket containing 11 of the most *beautiful* bull terrier puppies you have ever seen. They represented a small fortune when sold to carefully screened expectant pet owners.

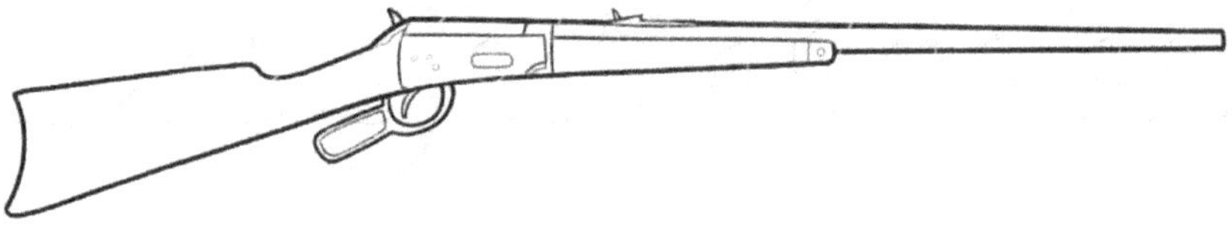

# THE HUNT

It seemed like the ideal day for our annual hunt. The crisp fall days were over and the brilliant orange and gold vine maple leaves had fallen and were decaying on the ground. The shortened days with unpleasant cold wet weather had settled in. The stark-naked tree branches were the only contrast to the leaden winter skies. Our quarry would be hunkered down preparing to endure the long hard winter season ahead. Cabin fever was incubating in our minds and bodies, and we had been watching too much football. It was time to get out of the house.

"Let's do it differently this year. Let's take the horses." Fortified by a last mug of scalding coffee and folding down the ear flaps of our felt hats we left the comfort of the fire and trooped out to the barn to make our preparations. The horses seemed eager to escape the monotonous routine of eating and then waiting 12 hours for the next flake of hay to be dumped into their feeders. They actually lowered their heads making haltering easier and virtually self-loaded into the trailer. The dog sneaked into the back seat of the pickup hoping not to have been noticed and thus allowed to come along. We relented.

We made our list and checked it twice. We already knew who was naughty and nice. Gloves, long johns, insulated boots, Carhartt coveralls, plastic tarp, rope, dusters with winter liners, blankets to cool down haired up sweaty horses, and appropriate weapons in the saddle bags completed the list. The diesel barked reluctantly and we eased onto the county road on our way to a favorite trail in the Rider's Camp area. Spinning tires proved that Manastash Canyon Road was a sheet of ice so I stopped to chain up as a precaution since we were pulling the horse trailer. Checking all four corners before starting up again, I heard a quite hissing. "Shoot," I pretended to say. The trailer was getting a flat. After unloading the horses and getting the high lift jack dug out, I discovered that the handle was AWOL. *Someone* failed to put it back where it belonged. Smiling a little sheepishly, I improvised with the handle of the manure fork. I quickly changed the tire, loaded the horses for the third time, and we were headed deeper into the cold winter woods.

Needless to say, there was plenty of parking space available at the Manastash Rider's Camp and no one to check on my expired Discover Pass. It didn't take long to saddle up and get our gear stowed in the saddle bags and scabbard but getting our bulked-out bodies up into the saddle proved to be problematic. Where was that damned mounting block? Finally, we gathered up our reins and headed up the trail. I think the horses appreciated their bitless headstalls. There was a freezing cold strong steady wind in our faces and the dark horizon forebode more weather arriving. The foot of new snow made silent traveling almost possible. We admonished the dog to say close and she was more than willing to travel in the plowed path left by the horses.

After a half hour of silent riding squinting into the developing storm someone said, "Aren't we getting close? We found them last year just around this bend in the creek and across that old bridge." We dismounted, haltered the horses, and tied them in a thick grove of white fir where they were somewhat sheltered against the wind. We could make a better stalk on foot. Someone said, "You can smell 'em." We eased on up the trail, weapons at the ready, with the dog following silently in our footsteps shivering in anticipation. Whomp! I suddenly fell on my _____(rear). I had discovered the hard way that the footbridge deck must have been a sheet of ice. I heard a muffled guffaw from behind me and barely managed to refrain from saying something (that seemed very appropriate to me). The dog licked my face adding insult to injury. I struggled up, dusted wet snow off my ____ (rear) and nursed my bruised ego and wounded pride. I needed a mug of hot chocolate, a warm raison oatmeal cookie, and my *blankie.* After I somewhat regained my composure, we proceeded cautiously up the trail and peered ahead over a slight rise in the trail with our weapons at the ready.

And there they were; huddled together under a blanket of new snow. A sudden strong blast of arctic air shook snow off all the trees in the area creating a total white out. We turned our backs against the blizzard until the air cleared. Dusting snow off our cheeks and eyelashes, we slowly turned around and gasped in surprise and dismay at the sight before our eyes. "And what to our wondering eyes should appear?" They were practically naked!

The Spruce Budworm elves had practically defoliated every tree in our special Engelmann spruce Christmas tree grove. We threw down our weapons in disgust: the small hatchet and pruning saw. The tarp and rope (intended for use dragging our prize trophy tree out of the woods) remained bundled up and seemed to mock us with their uselessness. Our hunting party trudged back down the trail head down and shoulders slumping . The impatient horses didn't even nicker as we arrived, seeming to reproach us for our lack of success. At least they were eager to get back to the truck and in no time, we were stowing gear and blanketing steaming wet horses for the trip out. The defroster struggled to keep the windshield clear as I stopped at the top of an especially steep grade. I mumbled something incomprehensible as I got out to put drag chains on the trailer. At least I still had my head screwed on straight not wanting to skid off the deserted road in the middle of the winter. My mare seemed restless as I tightened the chain binders, and I eased inside the trailer compartment to check her out. She was in distress from a mild gassy colic. Could things get any worse?

Some banamine, very cold fingers and feet, slow walking up and down the silent frozen byway and our efforts were rewarded with the satisfying audible sound of a mare passing large volumes of gas. We laughed *in spite of ourselves.* We reloaded for the fifth time, and slowly crawled down out of the mountains. Was I ever glad I had chained up the trailer as well. I felt better having it follow us down the mountain instead of leading the way. Six hours after our departure we were safely back right where we started, but empty handed and treeless. The hunt had been a total failure.

A shot of whisky in hot chocolate helped our state of mind, and we reminisced about our adventure. We could almost imagine that the mule deer we had seen had been wearing sleigh bells, and one of them either had a cold or a case of red nose. The next day we endured the eight-mile trek into town to Bi-Mart where we bought our very first artificial Christmas tree. I thought I heard the bell ringing Santa Clause with his cast iron pot snicker a little when he saw our purchase. I tried to smile when I put in a little money.

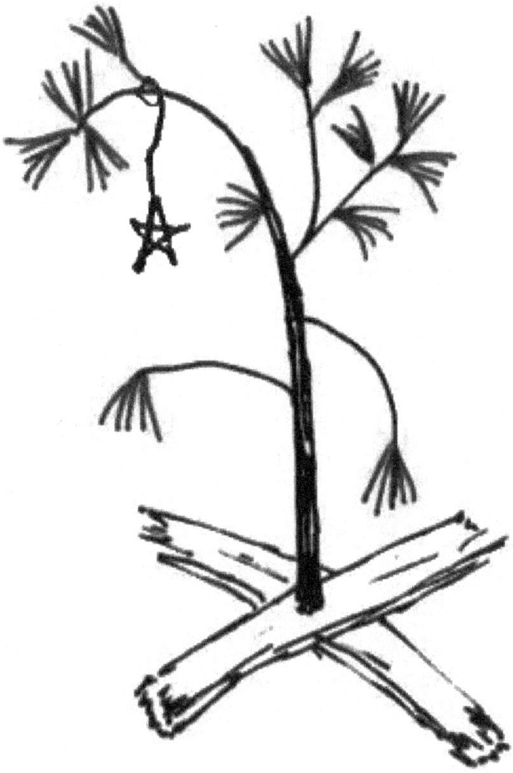

# NICE KITTY

While attending The College of Veterinary Medicine I provided care for a wonderful Standard Poodle after her orthopedic procedure. It didn't take long to fall in love with the breed - but not, necessarily, the haircut. After, discussing, consulting, and reading, my wife Linda and I made the life changing decision and commitment to get a puppy. We chose a black (shows dirt less) fuzz ball female (less behavior problems than with a male). Some chewed slippers, redesigned socks, modified upholstery, and a few accidental puddles later and Terra became our camping companion and scout dog for horse trail rides and pack trips. We mowed off her hair three times a year keeping her fancy pedigree secret. Without a poodle cut, most people seeing her in the mountains didn't know her regal ancestry.

It had been a typical long day; one among many in the life of a mixed animal veterinary practitioner. I loved my career as a veterinarian but it could be physically challenging and draining. It was early fall; the season of full moons, frosty pumpkins, and cold nights. One of each day's high points came in the evening when, after a hug from my wife, I was welcomed home by Queen Terra. She tried unsuccessfully to restrain herself, but was soon giving me a good licking. After a shower, some hot dinner, and a nap in front of the fireplace and TV with Terra at my feet, I stumbled off to bed. In the middle of the night Terra woke me up, from a dead to the world stupor, by barking frantically. Knowing she would never have an accident in the house, I ricocheted down the dark hall to let her out into the back yard. I stood there in the dark house shivering in my PJ's waiting, but Terra startled me fully awake with more insistent barking. So, I turned on the yard light to learn why.

I almost turned the light back off to erase the terrifying scene before my eyes. In the glare of the flood light Terra was barking and getting closer and closer and closer to......... a pretty black kitty with a white racing stripe down its back. My wrinkled nose and burning eyes said I was mistaken and it was already too late for preventative measures. The kitty's name was Pepe Le Pew. Having taken a full-frontal blast, poor Terra rolled frantically rubbing her face and burning eyes in the grass and piles of fall leaves seeking relief. Of course, she ducked and tried to squeeze between my legs to get back in the house to escape her torture. My wife smiled and said, "You were the one who let her out." Fortunately, my wife was married to a veterinarian who dutifully drove in to his office to get some *Skunk Off* - the only product that actually works. We dumped the garbage can out and gave it a cursory washing. Using it like an old-style laundry tub, but without the scrub board, we *refreshened* our dog. Using towels, the blow dryer, and a grooming comb, she was soon almost respectable enough to regain entrance into the house. We collapsed back into bed. It seemed like only seconds later the alarm went off signaling the start of a brand-new day. As my body awoke and warmed up that morning, I wondered if I too should have taken a bath in the garbage can. There always seemed to be a warm moist skunk following me around.

If a marriage is to survive, a veterinarian's wife needs to be flexible enough to withstand the inadvertent loss of sleep, the irregular hours, and the carefully prepared meals eventually ruined by microwave warming. Fortunately, my wife had a high tolerance level and only occasionally rolled over in the middle of the night to mumble, "It would sure be nice to sleep with a man who doesn't smell quite so skunky."

Sometimes sleepwalking events are forgotten or perhaps never remembered at all. Something similar must have happened to me, because two weeks later, Terra woke us up again in the middle of the night. Guess what? I let her out AGAIN, not realizing my mistake until she continued barking frantically. I heard my wife behind me groan, "Nooo! Not again!" We turned on the light expecting the worst. Terra was indeed barking determinedly at a skunk, but from a very calculated safe distance of 25 feet. The skunk was hurriedly exiting our floodlit back yard escorted from a long safe range by our (exceedingly intelligent) dog Terra. The skunk's tail was cocked and loaded but never did fire. Who says you can't teach an old dog new tricks. People, however, are sometimes slower learners. I think that garbage can still has the faint sweet cloying smell of skunk.

# GOOD STEW

Stu Bledsoe was a gentleman farmer in Kittitas County in the 40's, 50's, and 60's. His boots were usually polished and his brown felt hat was clean but he could get down and grubby like the rest of us. He was the third generation to cattle ranch on Wilson Creek Road on old family ground that is now called the Lazy Ed Ranch.

Summer range land included what is now Sun East and ran from the Highline Canal well up into the timber and from Wilson Creek Road almost over to Reecer Creek Road. Governor Albert Rossellini appointed Stu to be Director of the Washington State Department of Agriculture in the 1960's. When the US 9$^{th}$ District Court Boldt decision allocated half of the fisheries harvest to Washington State Native Americans, a totally new paradigm for dealing with fish and natural resources was necessary. Stu was deeply involved in the Washington Timber, Fish, and Wildlife (TFW) Agreement of 1978 which developed guidelines to deal with these new issues. He had a gift for gab and could schmooze with the best of them. He served our state well as a leader, politician, and consensus builder. He was grandfather to WSU's star football quarterback Drew Bledsoe who finished his NFL career with the Boston Patriots and is now a vintner in the lower valley.

Stu loved to hunt, perhaps even more than he liked politics. I suspect it was not so much to put meat on the table but for the camaraderie of the elk hunting camp. He loved the planning and logistics for the camp and felt it was his reward after all the fall cattle work was completed. His camp was in the Naneum Canyon near the junction of Boulder Creek Road, Swift Creek Road, and the main Naneum Creek Road. However, the Naneum was closed to the public being the watershed for the city of Ellensburg. Taylor Logging Company had the contract to log the old growth Ponderosa Pine native to the canyon. Chet Taylor was the father of Mickey Taylor, who was part owner of the race horse Seattle Slew. Stu and Chet were good friends and thus Stu had access to the key and the connections to use the locked Naneum logging roads to set up the camp.

It was sometime in the mid 1940's. Fall came early and winter came hard that year and the endless job of spreading feeder hay out in the fields for the cow herds began early. The ridges surrounding the valley were all white and the smell of wood burning stoves was always on the wind. The snow in the high country was soon deep and the deer and elk were driven down early by the weather into their winter range. Prospects for a successful hunt were excellent and local businessmen and ranchers were hoping they would be invited to Stu's hunting camp. This was before the era of 4WD vehicles and only military surplus and chained up ranch vehicles could negotiate the icy rutted roads to the camp.

Stu always planned everything. Invited hunters only had to bring their rifle and personal gear. Stu had the saddle horses, pack horses, food, kitchen tent, sleeping tents, and a huge cache of firewood. Scotch and Bourbon were also in adequate supply. Everyone met beforehand in the ranch barn and the potbellied stove glowed red and the hunting stories flowed. After loading up, it took an hour of bouncing, gear grinding, and spinning tires to get to the camp. The bourbon was already disappearing and a happy group tramped into the kitchen tent. A ranch hand had left early to get the stoves going and the tents warmed. Someone said, "What's for dinner?" Stu looked stunned. He had neglected to arrange for one extremely important item: the cook. There was usually some non-hunter more than willing to cook three meals a day for the hungry hunters in trade for the experience, comradery, and the free Bourbon. This year the cook position had gone unfilled.

Someone said, "Stu! You said you would provide everything but our personal gear. It's your camp. I guess you'll have to do the cooking. We might help out a little with the dishes."

Stu was embarrassed at his oversight and agreed to do most of the cooking until a cook could be shanghaied. "I'll cook but if anybody bitches, even a little, guess what their next job will be."

Hunting was good, tags were being filled, and Stu was totally occupied putting food on the table but he was also getting pretty desperate. He was so busy filling empty bellies that there was no time for him to hunt. The plan he formulated was soon evident. He burned the vegetables, added too much salt to the biscuits, made lumpy gravy, and even watered down the Bourbon but no one dared to complain. Not a peep! He had to get up by 5 a.m. to start the fires and get breakfast going. The promise to help with the dishes had been soon forgotten and paper plates didn't exist yet.

One morning before anyone was awake, a desperate Stu slipped out to the horse corral and gathered up some fresh road apples. He had to be fast or they would melt into the snow and disappear. It was hot cake morning and it was customary to add surprise items to the batter so Stu mixed up a large batch and added this predigested salad. Soon sleepy, grubby hunters itchy in their long woolen union suits were gathered at the breakfast table unconsciously gulping coffee and stuffing hotcakes into their mouths. Stu hid in the shadows behind the stove to watch the results of his efforts. There were quizzical looks, sideways glances, and some general uneasiness, coughing, and clearing of throats. Conversation was noticeably absent. Finally, someone cautiously said, "Stu, these hotcakes taste like horse shit, but they sure are good." The next meal eager volunteers lined up to take a turn at the stove and Stu soon got his bull elk. I suspect the rack of antlers is still gathering dust somewhere in the hay loft of the old ranch horse barn.

**Buddy**

# DO YOU BELIEVE IN MIRACLES

It had been a long exhausting week. Even Saturday was a full day of farm calls and office visits. When the morning sun came glaring through my bedroom window on that Sunday morning in the fall, I rolled over and hoped to continue catching up on missed sleep. It was not meant to be! About 7 a.m. the phone rang. I picked it up and tried to sound cheerful but I could only croak out, "Hello." At first, I wondered if there was anybody on the other end of the land line because there was only silence. Then I heard an incoherent voice, like someone choking or strangling, followed by silence again. When the voice came back again I was finally able to distinguish at least one word: "Buddy." Then the old memories came flooding back and I knew who was on the telephone. Here's how it all came about.

I was a recently graduated veterinarian full of enthusiasm and eager to test my newly acquired skills. I was doing relief work at a local veterinary clinic allowing the other doctors each to take summer vacation time. I planned to join a practice in British Columbia, Canada that fall as soon as I cleared immigration paperwork. This gave me a perfect opportunity to work in the interim and to gain practical experience.

Around the hospital they called them Bob and his Buddy. Bob was a senior student finishing his outdoor recreation degree at our local university. Buddy was a lanky tail wagging black Labrador cross with a permanent grin who had been rescued from our local animal shelter. Bob spent all his free time backpacking, canoeing, and pursuing other outdoor recreational activities. Buddy was his constant companion and partnered with Bob in all his adventures. On a cool Saturday morning in the previous September when I was still a veterinary student, Bob had been out jogging when Buddy got hit by a passing car. The car stopped and rushed them in to our veterinary hospital where Buddy was examined. He did not seem to be seriously injured except for difficulty breathing. An X-ray revealed two cracked ribs and severe bruising on his chest and abdomen but no other apparent serious problems were identified at that time.

Over time Buddy recovered and began his recuperation. As fall and winter set in conditions were not ideal for so much outdoor activity and Bob was busy with his studies. Thus, Buddy was able to spend the rest of the winter mainly indoors and gradually getting stronger.

Spring finally came and the winter's snow started slowly melting away. Bob and his Buddy begin easing into walks and hikes to get themselves back into shape. Finally, they were ready for their first major spring backpack trip up into the still snowy valleys of our Cascade Mountain foothills. Bob said that Buddy seemed to be struggling a little bit on the short hike Friday evening but he attributed it to the lack of exercise over the winter. On Saturday morning after an instant breakfast cooked on a Primus stove they stuffed the sleeping bag and tent into their pouches and Bob and Buddy worked their way further into the mountains. Suddenly Buddy collapsed and was too exhausted to even stay on his feet. His pulse was racing and his breathing was fast, short, and extremely labored. He was unable to travel at all. Bob wasn't certain what to do but in desperation dumped his pack contents under a tree and put Buddy in the now empty backpack. He raced down the valley to his car and ultimately to our office.

That's where I came into the picture. I was the duty veterinarian on that Saturday morning when Buddy was rushed in the front door. I got supplemental oxygen going and carefully eased Buddy onto the X-ray table. The results were pretty scary. There was something else in his chest making it impossible for his lungs to properly inflate. The history of his previous injury and the appearance of the X-ray told me that he had a diaphragmatic hernia. When he had been hit by the car the previous fall the pressure on his abdomen had forced his spleen and stomach through a tear in his diaphragm and into the thoracic cavity. The damaged diaphragm and the presence of these other structures in his chest made it impossible for the lungs to function properly and also greatly impaired blood circulation to these organs. The hike had aggravated the condition and left him in desperate condition.

Realizing I was in over my head, I called in the other senior doctors for consultation. Case records tell us that if the condition is identified and surgically corrected soon after the injury, the odds of survival are reasonable. However, if the injury is old from some time in the past, the lungs have been unable to function properly and the blood oxygen levels reach dangerously low levels. These animals are terrible surgical candidates and many of them don't even survive induction of anesthesia, let alone surgery.

We discussed the surgical risk and odds of survival with Bob. He said, "I don't have a lot of money but Buddy is my best friend. I have to do everything I can to help him." We didn't know about BFF back in the pre-cell phone era but Buddy fit the description.

My two older more experienced veterinary mentors both said, "He will never survive the surgery. You need to put him down." Bob overheard these comments and his eyes immediately filled with tears which streamed down his cheeks.

He asked me, "Will you at least try?"

I said, "Well, if we can get him on the surgery table we have at least a fighting chance." Against the other doctor's recommendations, I agreed to make an attempt. They reluctantly agreed to back me up giving me raised eyebrow looks of, "Are you sure you know what you are doing?" I encouraged Bob to go out for coffee and call in every half hour for an update.

Anticipating the worst, we prepared him for open chest procedure, should it be necessary. I gave him 20% of the recommended dose of anesthetic and watched his eyes slowly close as his breathing slowed and then stopped! A stethoscope quickly revealed that his heart had stopped as well. He was clinically dead! Our team of surgeons flew into action and we quickly opened his chest to apply hand massage to his flaccid heart. We injected epinephrine and miraculously his heart began beating again. The anesthesia machine allowed us to provide mechanical ventilation since he couldn't breathe on his own with an open chest cavity.

The stomach and spleen had been displaced so long that they were more or less glued (adhesions) in his chest. We had to gently coax them free and return them to their normal location in the abdomen. We repaired the tear in the diaphragm, wired shut the man-made opening in his sternum, and sutured the incision in the abdomen. The lungs had been partially collapsed for months but you don't attempt to immediately inflate them like a balloon. The body will gradually evacuate the air from the chest and the lungs will gradually expand themselves to normal size.

But now we had another potential crisis on our hands called reperfusion injury. The heart attempts to return normal circulation to these organs which ironically causes a massive inflammatory response. It was little understood then and still difficult to treat to this day. But Buddy was obviously a survivor and we were finally able to put him in our warmed recovery kennel. However, his recovery from the anesthetic was unusually prolonged due to reduced kidney and liver function. Finally, late in the evening he started to revive. Bob had no place else to go so we let him curl up on a pile of freshly laundered dog blankets in the corner of the recovery ward with instructions to call if there were any questions. By morning Buddy was stronger and more alert and even wagged his tail and licked Bob's face. He was able to eat a little bit of soft food and stand. However, there was one more huge problem. He was blind!

His brain had been deficient and finally deprived of adequate oxygen. Amazingly, it mostly recovered except, inexplicably, for the optic center. Over the next few days as his recovery progressed, he tripped and bumped around the hospital but rather quickly seemed to strengthen and compensate with his other senses and could cautiously navigate his way around.

Bob got his degree and graduated that spring with his parents and his tail wagging non-seeing eye dog in the audience. He moved to the west side of Washington State for a job in recreation at a community college. He was totally dedicated to his best friend and realized Buddy would need his life-long support. Buddy was able to jog with Bob, his seeing eye person, and even go on easy hikes.

Now fast forward to the following fall and the morning when I got the strange phone call. Bob had a daylight basement apartment which opened up through sliding glass doors to a backyard of lawn and trees. That morning he had taken Buddy for a potty break in the backyard, and then returned him to the apartment for a shared breakfast of scrambled eggs and sausage. Then Bob went out into the backyard to read the Sunday paper in the morning sunshine. He happened to look back towards the house and saw Buddy standing in the open doorway. Buddy looked up and obviously saw and recognized Bob. He wagged his tail vigorously and came bounding out into the backyard. He dodged around the fake fountain and the lawn gnomes and crashed into Bob knocking him off his lawn chair. Dancing, hugging, and tail thrashing, Buddy began licking hot tears off Bob's face. And that's when I got the strange early morning Sunday phone call.

# NICE MOMMY COW

"Sold," said the auctioneer. "For $.46. You might want to ask Doc over there in the back row why she still has stitches in her side." I was at the sales yard doing health checks on some auction cattle and there was no way to escape the friendly questioning when the sale ended. This is how it came about.

"We've got a mommy cow trying to have a baby," said the disembodied voice on the phone.

"What kind?" I mumbled.

"A white one," was the answer.

"I meant what breed," I said.

"I think it's a Charlene or Charlie or something like that," was the answer.

"Charolais?" I answered.

"Yes," was the relieved reply. It was 2 a.m. and a nasty freezing rain was falling. I wasn't particularly eager to crawl out from between my warm blankets. The caller's lack of cattle knowledge turned on my mental smoke alarm.

"Do you have her caught?" I asked.

"No," was the answer.

"Well, when you have her caught so I can work on her, call me back and I will be right out," I grumbled.

I waited groggily for the phone to ring and finally relapsed into a deep coma again. Two hours later the phone again startled me awake. "Sorry for the delay," the voice said, "But we had to take the owner to the hospital because the cow broke his leg. But we did finally manage to get the cow into the old barn."

It wasn't long until I slithered to a halt on the ice in their driveway. They explained that they had purchased the house and barn and a few acres of an old dairy farm intending to fix it up. Everyone said they needed to have a few cows on their "Farm." So, they went to the livestock auction and bought a pretty white beef heifer. They escorted me into a dusty cobweb filled old flat dairy barn; the kind with gutters behind the stanchioned cows to catch the poop. Off in the dark of a far corner I could just make out the faint silhouette of a two horned, one tailed, four-legged ghost. I wasn't born with a rope in my hand so I wasn't typically very handy with a lariat. Every time I stepped into the pen the cow treated me like a matador only without the red cape. It's pretty hard to push a cow away using a rope for a stick.

Off in another corner of the barn was an old 1948 model 8N Ford tractor. "Does it still run?" I asked. "I think we can get her started," was the answer. After some coaxing, silent swearing, starter grinding, and a cloud of blue smoke, I was mounted on my four wheeled motorized roping steed. When the cow attacked the rear tire, I deftly dropped a rope over her head and then drove several times clockwise around a post in the middle of the barn to secure her. The city folks watched carefully from the other side of the fence while I attempted to extract the calf. Without my realizing it, the cow did several reverse turns counterclockwise around the post, unwound herself, and suddenly had about 20 feet of slack in the lariat. Before I could escape she had knocked me down and was rolling me across the barn floor with her nose like I was a peanut in a race. Fate must have been on my side for she ran out of rope and I managed to escape on my hands and knees. Fortunately, before my escape from certain death, I had been able to determine that she had a large calf and it was unlikely that it could be delivered naturally. Deciding to do a C-section on my new best friend was a foregone conclusion.

Usually, when you do a C-section, you administer a local anesthetic at the incision site and do the surgery with the patient standing. I reluctantly cast aside the option of using a large sledge hammer. A spinal anesthetic was more appropriate in that the cow would be at my mercy fully immobilized stretched out flat on the ground. We clipped the winter haircoat off her side, scrubbed the area thoroughly, incised the skin and muscle, and then opened up the uterus. It took two of us to pull the huge calf from the surgical hole in the cow's belly. Amazingly, it was alive with a strong heartbeat and good respiration stimulated by tickling his nostril with a straw. Then the uterus was stitched closed, the muscles sutured, and the skin incision reapposed.

We cleaned up and stowed my instruments and tools and rescued my rope from around the cow's neck. We made certain beforehand that she was still not able to get up and resume her attack mode. I waited to be sure that the cow eventually got up and was delighted to see her stagger over and lick the new born calf. I told the owner's wife as I drove out the driveway, "You can take the stitches out in two weeks." It goes without saying that they never did take those stitches out.

That fall when the last summer grass was gone, the cow, with her stitches still intact, and her beautiful large bull calf at her side went to the cattle auction and sold for $.46/lb.

# HAS ANYONE SEEN MY HORSE

After I completed my Army service in the spring of 1969, I needed a summer job to tide me over until WSU pre-veterinary classes started in the fall. The USFS District Ranger saw me on the street one day and after chatting for a few minutes asked, "Do you want a job?" I had attended high school with his son and daughter and had worked for him previously as the trail crew foreman just after high school. "I don't think our present wilderness ranger is doing well living by himself in the woods. Kind of like reverse cabin fever," he said. "I expect one Monday he won't show up. The early high mountain deer hunt is coming up and we need someone for fire patrol. If he doesn't come back do you want the job?"

"Yes," I said without hesitation. I had been working at the local vegetable food freezing plant and needed to be rescued. I was not particularly suited to the endless mindless nature of the work.

Only a few days later on a Monday the telephone rang. It was Ranger Warren. He said, "Bob left a message on the answering machine this morning and said he couldn't take it anymore. How soon can you be ready to go?"

"Is tomorrow morning soon enough?" I eagerly replied. "I can supply my own horse," I added.

"Great! I'll have Lynn guide you in to show you the camp," said the Ranger.

By 10 a.m. the next morning we were on horseback and on our way up the trail to the Wilderness Ranger's Camp near Waptus Lake. I was riding my own horse and Lynn was riding Chief, a Forest Service saddle horse, and we were leading two pack mules. Chief was a huge half draft buckskin who had a mind of his own and was king of the corral. His size and unflappability actually seemed to help keep peace within the forest service corral because none of the other animals dared to challenge him. He had been around for at least 10 years and had been on all the trails in the district. It was 11 miles into the camp and we arrived there in the late afternoon. The camp had a tent frame with a sheepherder stove and two cots, an outhouse, an outdoor fire pit for cooking, a hitching rail, and a corral.

After we unpacked the mules and unsaddled the horses, Lynn said, "We can just turn the stock loose. We've got the grain here and Chief will just hang around camp. The mules will never leave the horses." Lynn usually rode a desk or a pickup truck and not a horse and didn't appear to have an excess of horse experience.

So, I asked, "Are you sure?"

"No worries," was his confident reply.

"Ok," I said. "But I'm keeping mine tied up close to camp." Lynn couldn't cook but cooking over an open fire was something I really enjoyed. So, I buried potatoes at the edge of the fire to bake, got some cornmeal muffins going in the Dutch oven, made a green salad, and put some chuck steak on the fire to grill. After stuffing ourselves we had a cold Olympia beer for desert. Sleep came quickly as soon as we crawled into our warm sleeping bags. The sensation of a pack rat scampering over my sleeping bag trying to get into the food box woke me up once in the middle of the night. The quiet hoot hooting of a spotted owl was the last thing I heard before going back to sleep.

I woke in the morning at daylight, shivered into my Levi's, and kicked the fire together. My horse nickered anxiously, but the other three were nowhere to be found. The only sign of them was a few piles of cold horse poop and an empty torn-up feed sack. After a quick cold breakfast, we followed the footprints out of camp and down the trail expecting that they had traveled all 11 miles back to the trailhead. It was going to be a long walk out for cowboy Lynn. However, at a junction in the trail the horse's footprints unexpectedly turned up valley deeper into the mountains toward a high mountain pass.

Lynn smiled and said sheepishly, "It looks like I was wrong about the horses. I'll start hiking out to the trailhead."

I said, "I have to patrol toward that pass anyway, so I'll go back to camp and load my saddlebags and ride out that way."

Half an hour later my horse and I scrambled up through narrow sharp switchbacks between cliffs where mountain goats feed in the spring. Eventually we arrived in the Waptus Pass area of scattered soggy grassy meadows, thick patches of silver fir, good spring water, and also clouds of mosquitoes. The horse tracks disappeared between the trees into the meadows and I spent several hours sweating, swatting mosquitoes, and trying to locate them. I suspect the animals had their bellies full of grass and were resting hidden away in a thicket somewhere avoiding the mosquitoes. Lacking the tracking skills of a mountain man, I decided to continue patrolling on to a trout filled lake where hunters were known to camp. I planned to come back later in the day to continue my search. I arrived at the hunter's camp to find it empty but a camp fire still burning. I put the fire out and continued on down the trail. A couple of miles later I met the hunters and cautioned them about the campfire and asked if they would keep their eyes open for the missing stock.

I returned to the meadows and again tried to find tracks from the missing horses. I hunted until almost dark and had to finally admit failure. Fortunately, I could trust my horse to find his way down through the cliffs in almost total darkness. He must have been able to read my mind for when we came to the trail junction he chose to return to the camp instead of continuing down the valley to the trailhead. The tread traveled alongside a noisy stretch of the river before crossing over. In the total darkness, I only knew we were on the bridge because I could hear the clip clop of my horse's feet on the wooden deck. After locating my headlamp, I unsaddled my horse, put on his nose bag and a cow bell, and tied him to the hitching rail alongside the tent. That way I could hear him through the night and occasionally talk to him in the darkness so that he would not feel totally abandoned.

I slept in a little late the next morning and gave my horse some time for some extra breakfast pellets. We continued patrolling for the rest of the week up two other glacial valleys with small cirque lakes at their terminus. The days passed quickly but I continued to fret and wonder what had become of the livestock. On Friday, as my week ended I rode back down the valley hoping to find horse foot prints headed in the right direction. The only signs I saw were deer tracks and a pile of purple berry poop left by a bear who would soon be hibernating for the winter.

We had left messages at the two possible trailheads asking hunters and hikers to be on the lookout. Lynn took considerable ribbing from the rest of the office staff who said, “I understand you've been doing quite a bit of hiking lately." My patrolling took me elsewhere and almost two weeks passed. There had even been a light dusting of snow in the high peaks. Finally, a local hunter familiar with the area phoned the Forest Service office stating that as he was packing out of his hunting camp he spotted a horse and two mules. He tried to catch them but they just toyed with him and trotted off into the timber.

My job was finished for the year but realizing that winter was closing in the Ranger asked if I would go on a horse hunting trip. On a Saturday morning I packed my saddlebags with snacks, a little grain, and three halters and prepared for a long twenty-six-mile solo ride. I left before sunrise and three hours later arrived in the pass area. I found where the stock had been grazing and even found manure piles under trees where they had apparently spent the nights. Again, I searched knowing that the animals were in the vicinity, but I could not find them.

Had the horses finally realized that their summer holiday was over, and that they needed to get down out of the mountains before winter snowfall began? Perhaps this was the case, for as I left the pass area and started down the other side of the ridge, horse tracks suddenly appeared in the trail. It was late in the afternoon and I still had about 14 miles to ride. It was well after dark on an overcast moonless night when I arrived at the trailhead and traveled a short distance to the government corrals. In the total darkness, I could hear and just make out a horse and two mules picking at some of the old hay left in the manger. I'm sure that the next day when we got them back to the main corrals at the ranger station, Chief said to the other horses and mules, "Those silly humans never would have been able to find us. It was getting boring out there and we just decided it was finally time to come home."

I spent six more summers at that camp but declined using Chief as a packhorse. It would have been embarrassing if the packhorse knew the country better and proved to be smarter than the person using him.

# FREE PUPPY

The wind was blowing hard as it often does in these parts. It could make the weather stripping around the door frame hum and moan and the glass shift in the window frames when hard gusts hit. The door flew open when a pet owner came in and a strong blast of wind scattered paperwork and half-a-dozen leaves across the tiled reception room floor. Suddenly a small fuzzy apricot dust mop bounced across the room chasing them. It killed two, squatted briefly to leave a small puddle, and then barked demandingly to be picked up. This was my introduction to Peppermint Patty's Sister, a twelve-week-old standard poodle puppy. When I lifted her up on the exam table she said "Hello" by giving me a big wet kiss right on the nose when I foolishly got within range of her licker. "We imported her all the way from upstate New York," her owners proudly said. "She's a Royal Standard Poodle." Royals are exceptionally large standard poodles reaching weights of up to 80 lbs.

Bob and Mildred Goodenough had brought her in for the first of her puppy vaccinations. Bob said, "The name Patty didn't seem sufficiently distinguished to us so we decided to call her

Elizabeth. She already acts like the queen of the house." Bob explained, in a self-important way, that Mildred would soon be getting a total knee replacement and inasmuch as he was usually busy, they got Elizabeth as a companion for Mildred during her recovery. What for me was pure joy and delight struck me as being pretty high energy for a couple in their mid-seventies.

In the course of finishing her puppy vaccination series and doing the surgery to spay her, we got to know Liz pretty well. If you tried to tell her what to do, she had a way of looking at you and saying, "You can't tell me what to do," and she would ignore you and dash off to investigate something more important if only to prove her point. However, she was soon prancing back because she expected you to want to share her discovery.

A few months later, we got a disturbing call from Bob. He said, "Mildred had her knee surgery but the recovery is going a little slow. I have been doing all the housework, taking care of Mildred, and trying to control this crazy puppy. Two walks a day and she still demands more attention. This has obviously been more than I can handle. I had some chest pains and the doctor said I had had a mild heart attack. We found someone to do the housework and help me take care of Mildred but we came to the sad conclusion that this puppy is just too much for us. We knew that you have had standard poodles and wondered if you would be willing to take Elisabeth."

A quick phone call to my wife confirmed my instinctive response. We missed having a big smart but silly dog around the house and to accompany us on our outdoor adventures. That evening we drove out to the Goodenough's house to collect Elizabeth and her bed, blanket, food dish, and a huge basket of well chewed puppy toys. They seemed relieved to see her go. We were delighted.

Liz quickly adopted us and adapted our family routine to fit her world. She sniffed noses with the cats, occasionally consumed a little bit of fresh road apple salad from the barn, and checked out the tack room for any varmints or undesirables. This was her home and she loved it! We took her to the irrigation canal on a hot summer day and discovered that she could not swim. I waded out chest deep into the water carrying her with me. I supported her weight until she got her paddle wheels going and gradually let her down hoping to have her discover that she could actually swim. She paddled and splashed wildly with her front feet determined to prevent her *do* from getting wet. Then I discovered that her body was long enough that she had her back feet resting safely on the bottom of the canal and wasn't really swimming at all.

As the summer wore on she easily fit into our horse camping routine. She would scout ahead making sure the trail was safe for us and then run back to encourage us to keep up. She even accidentally discovered how to swim. She was a fishing fanatic. She learned to identify the clicking sound of line being pulled out of a fishing reel and would go absolutely bonkers. Once a fish was landed she wanted to capture it and retrieve it and we were, of course, afraid of her being snagged by the fishhook. Once when a hooked fish jumped and splashed, in her excitement she jumped into the lake to catch it. Too late she discovered the water was over her head and we almost had to jump into the water to save her. Somehow, her survival instincts kicked in and she managed to flounder her way back to shore. She shook herself off and looked back at us rather sheepishly with an embarrassed look on her face. However, we thought we heard her say, "Nothing to it. I knew how to swim all along." Life was good!

But then somebody threw us a curve ball. Cindy my receptionist said, "There's a guy out here with a list saying something about how you owe him some money." I'm sure my face transformed into a big question mark. I poked my head around the door frame to see Mr. Goodenough standing there with a self-righteous look stamped on his determined face.

I said, "I'll be right with you."

He said, "I don't have all day, you know." I joined him shortly and he shoved a piece of paper in my face.

It read:

| | |
|---|---|
| PURCHASE ELIZABETH | $750 |
| SHIPPING | $250 |
| VACCINATIONS | $60 |
| SPAY | $85 |
| TOTAL OWED ME | $1145 |

"You have my dog and I have nothing," he said.

"But I thought you gave her to us," I responded.

"Well, I changed my mind. Pay me what you owe or I'm taking my dog back," he growled. A cascade of arguments of fairness and reasonableness raced through my bewildered head. Showing uncharacteristic restraint, I bit my tongue and said nothing. If I opened my mouth who knows what would have come out. He kept growling like an old dog with a bone.

I took a deep cleansing breath and said, "I'll go write you a check." I don't think he heard what I said and just kept barking. I turned my back and just walked away. When I came back I handed him a check and said, "Please leave." He kept on talking about what I owed him. I turned away again and walked into the quiet darkness of my X-ray room.

After about 20 minutes Cindy peaked around the corner and said, "He's finally gone. I'm so sorry. You have appointments waiting."

At the end of the day I drove quietly home and gave Elizabeth a slow heartfelt hug and she, instinctively sensing my need, licked my face. Then I hugged my wife. She didn't lick my face. She did, however, ask, "What's wrong?" Over a shared beer I told her what happened. We sat quietly contemplating our navel, world peace, and the human animal bond. Finally, she asked, "Don't you have this weekend off?"

I said, "Yes."

She said," Let's load up the horses and take our four-legged daughter on a pack trip." And we did.

# YOU CAN'T KEEP A GOOD MAN DOWN

I think his official AKC name was something like Charlie's Runamuck, but we called him Trip, for reasons that will become obvious as you learn the rest of the story. He was a classic old style teddy bear chocolate Labrador Retriever. Do dogs smile? Well, he certainly displayed a big toothy grin. With a bear sized head, big soft ears, and dark expressive eyes that followed you everywhere, he belonged stretched out in front of a fireplace. If you sat down, he liked to lie against your feet knowing that he wouldn't get left behind that way. He weighed a lean 100lbs and was what I called a *two can a day* sized dog. He seemed to always smell good too, like the outdoors, unless, of course, he overate. Carl, his owner, and his father were bird hunters and had always had a good bird dog in the family. With Carl off to college, Dad had no one to hunt with, so he sent Trip off to fulfill the position of college roommate/chaperone. Perhaps Dad thought Trip would have a good steadying influence on Carl.

The first time I met Trip, he was in trouble. Carl loved his dog but wasn't always the best parent. When he got up about 6:30 in the morning he opened the door and let Trip out to 'take care of business'. Leash laws were for everyone else. Carl's rental house was across the street from my office and we often watched Trip do his morning rounds checking the trees and fireplugs for overnight messages, sniffing the bushes for late rising birds, and dodging the increasing morning traffic. Usually after about 30 minutes he was back home scratching at the front door.

But you guessed it. Trip got hit by a car. A frantic Carl burst through the waiting room door struggling to carry Trip in his arms. Trip had made it home with only a few scrapes but he was dragging his right front leg. An X-ray confirmed our worst fears showing that he had been hit in the shoulder and broken his humerus. Making matters worse was the fact that gentle pin pricks and pinches showed that Trip had no feeling in the front of his foot (equivalent to the back of our hand). Sadly, this confirmed that he had crushed or severed his radial nerve; the nerve that enabled him to dig or place his foot in your lap. We can fix bones but not destroyed nerves. With this nerve gone a dog drags his paw on the ground feeling no pain but gradually destroys it. You splint and wait a week in hopes that sensation will return but eventually there is no option but to take the leg off.

We performed the sad but necessary surgery late on a Friday morning, so that Carl would be able to provide weekend nursing care. I looked in on Trip during my lunch break and he was already standing on his three remaining legs wagging his tail with his usual toothy smile on display. What a guy! His recovery was uneventful and Carl pushed him home in a borrowed wheelbarrow. Leash walking was encouraged and 2 weeks later we saw Trip for suture removal. He quickly cleared lower office shelves of their contents with enthusiastic broad sweeps of his tail and barked his approval when asked if he *was ready to go*. Carl at that time explained that his dog had acquired a new name. His college beer drinking buddies said that his dog stood solid as a tripod and thus he was christened TRIP. A few generous laps of beer had provided confirmation. After pointed discussions about the reasons for leash laws and serious promises resulting *from having learned his lesson the hard way* we wished them well and sent them out the door. We were gratified to see Trip leading Carl on long walks to the nearby city park morning and evening, and even during lunch breaks from class.

But late summer turned to fall and fall turned to winter and winter turned to cold. Not the most ideal conditions for dog walking. It was still dark outside one morning when I arrived at my office to see Trip out taking himself for a walk. He had his winter coat on but having his horsepower reduced by 25% hadn't slowed him down at all. His communication network and been down for 3 months and he had a lot of smell mail to catch up on. I laughed about it with my staff but we reluctantly decided to *mind our own business* and hope for the best. Trip had acquired a reflective collar so he was at least visible in the dark when caught by car headlights.

Can lightning strike twice in the same place? I guess so if you live on a mountain top or let your dog run loose in the streets. Trip took another ride across the street in his wheelbarrow ambulance. This time it was his left rear leg (hock - equivalent to our ankle) which had been ground open by a tire against the pavement, exposing all the joint surfaces. Yes, it was ugly. Gut wrenching discussions about cost, payment, and predictions about Trip's mobility led to the decision to *do the best that we could.* The joint was beyond repair so we ankylosed (surgically froze or locked) it in a position where it would be somewhat useful. His irrepressible spirit was quickly on display again for once he was helped up onto his two good legs, he was ready to go on his rounds. When he got tired he would lean against a tree, telephone pole, or car tire which was convenient since he could deliver or check for smell messages at the same time. It was difficult, however, to deliver his reply messages at the proper height on bushes. As healing continued he learned to use the stiff leg to get up and for balance but once he got going he preferred to travel on two legs moving like a hobby horse. We emphasized the importance of diet and weight control to maximize his mobility. The poor guy was thus always starving but still smiled and wagged his tail.

Since Mom and Dad were the counselors and bankers throughout all of Trip's difficulties, we had gotten to know them and enjoy their company. They stopped in one spring afternoon two years later to chat. They said, "We fixed Trip up with a tasseled mortar board graduation hat and took him to attend Carl's graduation ceremony this morning. He smiled and thumped his tail on the ground all the way through and seemed to recognize Carl when he whooped from the platform. Trip did his job helping Carl grow up and graduate. I guess we'll take him home for a well-earned retirement."

**TRIP**

**ROSA**

# THE PRINCESS

Rosa wasn't supposed to last this long. But here she is! A long-haired Chihuahua princess. Long lion colored well-groomed coat, foxy erect ears, bright eyes, nails trimmed and buffed, sparkling white teeth and a ferocious bark guaranteed to chase away the most dangerous stuffed animal. She's an undercover foot warmer for her Dad at night and a licensed couch guard during the day. Her throne at the top of the couch back cushion gives her command over the domain of all her human and canine subjects. But the story had a less compelling beginning.

It was sort of a family business. Auntie ran the factory which sometimes had as many as 70 carefully selected employees, and her nephew Robert was the business manager/salesman. They ran a puppy mill, in the best sense of the word. The dogs were all loved, fed, and well cared for and also had the run of Auntie's house. Robert did the grooming, training, showing, and salesmanship. I suspect he missed his true calling as a hairdresser.

Pregnancy is tough on little dogs. Their beautiful haircoat deteriorates and falls out. They struggle with nutrition for if they eat too much they vomit and if they eat too little they get skinny. They need to snack 24/7. Whelping (vet language for giving birth) is even worse. Small litters sometimes lead to mismatched puppy size with one occasionally too large to be delivered normally. That's when we usually saw Robert and Auntie. They lived an hour away and the calls came late at night after a bitch (momma dog) had been struggling to deliver. Sometimes we were able to deliver the puppies naturally but all too often a C-section was required. This posed a cruel dilemma for our clients since they were running a business and they couldn't give all their profits to us.

Such was the case with Rosa. It must have been after midnight when they brought her in disheveled and exhausted, having been trying to deliver puppies since noon. The haunting look in her eyes said she had given up and had put her life in our hands. An X-Ray confirmed that she had one overlarge puppy inside obviously impossible to deliver. "What a shame," said Robert. "She's out of our best stud but she gave us no live pups out of her last litter. She's obviously not a breeder and we can never get her in shape for the show ring." There was a long painful silence before Robert said, "I guess we need to put her down." I looked at my associate to see slumped shoulders and downcast eyes. Then she looked at me and I could see the sadness in her eyes but also a questioning look. There was another painful silence and then I said to Robert, "How about we trade the bill for the dog?" I could see the relief on his face when he eagerly said, "Fantastic."

This was my associate's first C-section so I stood by to assist. The procedure went perfectly except we found a large ugly monster puppy with a lethal heart defect. Abnormal circulation had led to a bloated fluid filled body cavity. After recovery, Rosa went home with her new owner (my associate) to be carefully attended to in the family ICU (bedroom). (I don't think she ever relinquished those sleeping arrangements.) Two weeks later a new Rosa was revealed. She came in for stitch removal and a greet and meet with the rest of the staff. She had blossomed into a golden bouncy fluff ball dodging feet and tugging at shoelaces. We got weekly reports on her progress and antics.

Six months later on a Saturday evening I got a phone call from Robert. "Quick! Turn on your TV to the Westminster Dog Show at Madison Square Garden! They're starting the toy classes." A loud click followed by silence indicated that he had hung up. We watched the Min Pins, Maltese, Pomeranians, and Tea Cup Poodles and finally the Chihuahuas. The class was narrowed down to two males and a female and finally a defiantly proud fluff of a male prancing around the ring was chosen best of class. The phone rang again. "That was Rosa's sire! I couldn't get away myself so I sent him with another trainer to the show in New York. I couldn't be prouder. You realize that you are the owner of a dog with royal blood line!" I know somewhere there is a carefully preserved newspaper clipping.

Years pass and Rosa is in trouble. She's having seizures and total collapse almost to the point of paralysis. An adrenal disease called Addison's? Brain tumor? Testing leads us to suspect GME, an immune disease that can affect the brain. A trip to the College of Veterinary Medicine confirms the diagnosis and a grave prognosis is given. Her chances of survival are slim.

Years pass and Rosa is still undeniable very much here. What do those specialists know? There have been ups and down and several life-threatening crises. But she still plays tug-of-war with her smaller cousin and reigns over her empire from the back of the couch. Intruders pass over the threshold under threat of dismemberment. The last time I saw her I thought I heard her say, "You guys wouldn't give up on me when I needed help so I am going to hang around as long as I can to watch over you. Tu perro. vive!"

We lost Rosa in 2017. She is greatly missed. I know all her stuffed animal toys now have little wings.

# HE DID WHAT

Why do the strangest calls come in the middle of the night? At least it wasn't *dark and stormy*. The clock said 2 a.m. when the bedside phone rang. After years of practice I could wake up, pick up the phone before the first ring stopped, and mumble a semi-intelligent "Hello." My wife seemed able to sleep right through it or did a great job pretending to be asleep. A voice said, "Can you come out? Our horse Pete fell into a hole?" I got up and dressed. I would later find out that I had put my T-shirt on inside out. At least my fly was zipped up.

The Thompsons lived five winding miles up in one of the river carved basalt canyons, so, I put my truck on autopilot and pulled out onto the county road. The full harvest moon illuminated the brilliant fall foliage of Indian summer and made the wakeup call seem less intrusive. A nice 4-point buck deer in the headlights startled me awake as I drove down the lane to their small hobby farm.

The automatic back-yard light switched on and Bob came out wearing pajamas and slippers. "I had to get up because our old Springer Spaniel Blondie needs to be let out in the middle of the night to do her thing. I always check first for skunks but looking around I couldn't find Pete. We had put him into our fenced garden to eat the left-over corn and vegetable tops. I got a flashlight and walked out barefoot to look and finally found him in a hole in the ground." We walked back to the garden to observe that Pete, an old piebald paint gelding, had fallen through the rotten lid of an old abandoned cesspool. A cesspool is the precursor to the modern septic tank and was a large concrete box often covered with a wooden plank lid.

Pete was standing quietly, relatively unharmed, amidst dirt and broken boards with only the tips of his ears showing. He nickered. We gave him some grain and more veggies to keep him occupied while we pulled out the lumber and debris. There was just enough room to work beside Pete in the dark hole although it was a little claustrophobic being in there with 1000 lbs. of muscle. I tried not to think about the former function of the structure. Closer examination revealed only a few minor scrapes and there was certainly nothing wrong with his appetite. He even deposited a few fresh new *apples* in the appropriate receptacle.

We pondered how to get him out. Sedation/anesthetic? 1000 helium balloons? A squadron of butterflies? The bucket on the neighbor's tractor? A tripod hoist with a block and tackle? All of which required devising a sling to fit under and around his belly. I've sometimes had used old carpet for this purpose but it takes time to manufacture. Someone joked and said, "Let's just feed him beans and let him float out."

The next suggestion also got a good laugh. "He's so old anyway. Why don't we just bury him where he is and get it over with?" A dim light bulb switched on in the back of my brain.

"That might just work," I said. Everybody laughed again. "I'm serious," I said. "If we fill the hole with dirt and he stays on top of the pile, he'll be lifted right out."

Two hours of sweaty shoveling, half a dozen blisters, and Pete calmly walked right out of the hole. He sidled over to the row of carrots and began biting off the tops as if to say, "What was all the fuss about." A small cheer arose.

Someone said, "That calls for a celebration. We just saved Pete from deep shit."

Bob said, "I have some cider that's already turning so let's finish it off." By the time the cider was gone and we had washed off with the garden hose, the sun was up and it was time to go to my office and start morning surgeries. I gave Pete a precautionary tetanus booster and pointed my truck toward town. The 4-point buck was just departing having gotten his fill of fallen apples. I again admired the colors of the alders and aspens along the creek bottom. I walked in to my surgery and my veterinary assistant said, “You sure look bright eyed and bushy tailed and ready to go this morning. You must have slept well.” I just smiled.

# WHAT TOOK YOU SO LONG

It was going to be the final trail ride of the season. There had already been a light skiff of snow on the ground which had melted quickly in the afternoon sun. The trail was soft and muddy but manageable nevertheless. The horses were already haired up for winter but were dancing and eager to go in the crisp fall air. Their shoes were long past the pull date but we thought we could surely squeeze another 20 miles out of them. Our Standard Poodle Liz had already self-loaded into the back seat of the truck ready to guide us on a ride into a high mountain river valley.

The parking lot was vacant when we pulled in. The woods were silent as we unloaded and saddled the horses. The usually noisy Douglas squirrels and Blue Jays were already settled in for the long winter ahead and were hiding quietly in their nests. The Tamarack needles were a brilliant yellow in the slanting sunlight.

Horses don't usually volunteer to trot when going away from the trailer but that was the case this day. Ears forward, head high, and steam rising from flared nostrils, up the trail they flew with us hanging on from the saddle. Liz, as usual, was already far up the trail. She would run forward out of sight to check for slow squirrels or anything else that caught her nose or eye, and then retrace her route to make sure that we were still safely coming along. If we traveled 10 miles with the horses she surely traveled at least 15. Her long lean body gobbled up the miles and she never seemed to get tired. On these rides, she sometimes reverted to her natural state: that of the very rare Black Footed Apricot Poodle which was the result of traveling over and through muddy terrain.

The trail dodged around strange sandstone formations intermingled with basalt dykes from 70 million years ago, as it climbed over a low hogback. The timber shifted from Douglas fir to Western red cedar as we passed through some small damp drainages and then to a large stand of Lodgepole Pine. There had been a small wildfire in that area a few years earlier and the dead stark black trees stood silhouetted against the sky. Liz kept racing on ahead and then trotting back to encourage the horses to move faster to keep up. We heard her bark excitedly as she flushed a grouse up into a nearby tree. It seemed like the grouse clucked mockingly as we passed underneath her branch.

We dropped off the north side of the ridge down to the whitewater river below. The trail was now in deep shadow as the low winter sun was hidden behind the southern ridge line. The initial two-mile hard climbing section was behind us and now we settled into a steady rhythm with the horses clicking off miles as we traveled upriver. There were waterfalls, stretches of white water, and quiet pools begging you to come back in the summer and fly fish. Some 15,000 years ago, glacial advance had etched long deep gouges in the ancient hard serpentinite rock. Trees were growing precariously from cracks in the rocks and bright green moss covered the surfaces. Five miles further up the trail we passed an old campsite some hundred feet off the trail at the edge of the river. We turned in to water the horses and have a snack before the return trip. We dismounted knowing that Liz had traveled on ahead but expected she would soon come back to check on us and to share our sandwiches and cowboy cookies.

When she didn't show up we became concerned and called her but to no avail. We only heard the echo of our own worried voices. We went back to check the trail only to find fresh dog footprints going the wrong way. In coming back to locate us she must have missed us down by the noisy river watering the horses. Apparently, she was using her nose to back-track us down river back to the truck.

Stowing our uneaten sandwiches in the horn bags, we quickly remounted and headed back down the trail. The horses obviously knew the direction back to the truck and needed no encouragement. We hoped that by traveling fast we would surely catch up with our confused dog. Trotting and even cantering when the terrain allowed, we flew back down the trail. Every time we crossed a stream we saw her footprints with the wet spots still expanding on the rocks. Did we see flashes of apricot hair disappearing ahead around bends in the trail or was it the dappling of the low angled early winter sun on the last of the alder leaves? Was that her wagging tail or just a branch waving in the breeze?

It doesn't take long to eat up the miles traveling 10 miles an hour. In only forty minutes we could look down the trail and see our truck in the deserted parking lot; but there was no tail wagging poodle. I think our hearts must have missed 5 beats. Where could she be? On down the road? *Rescued* by someone? Dinner for a cougar? Anxious thoughts raced through our heads. Weak kneed from the ride and from worry, we dismounted to collect ourselves. What should we do? Wait? Drive to the nearby resort? Go back up the trail? Call the sheriff? There really was no good answer.

Just then, Liz crawled out from her bed under the horse trailer, stretched, yawned, shook herself off, and said, "What took you guys so long? I could sure use a bite of beef jerky." We willingly shared some of our uneaten P&J sandwich.

**Elizabeth (Liz)**

# HERE KITTY KITTY

It seems that almost every location inhabited by humans is also home to stray or feral cats. Humans are not always good stewards for our feline friends. Cat DNA is not that far removed from that of their wild ancestors so abandoned domestic cats breed and try to survive in the periphery of humanity. Empty barns, abandoned buildings, any place with shelter can be a home for feral cats. They eat rodents but also prey on songbirds, suffer from infected wounds from fighting, and spread cat diseases among themselves. Historically, these poor creatures have been captured, and with the exception of a few young friendly ones, are humanely euthanized.

Unfortunately, once these wild populations have been trapped and eliminated, the affordable housing is vacant and new cats quickly move in. There had to be a better way, and thus the idea of TNR or trap, neuter, and release system slowly evolved beginning in the mid 1960's. Good Samaritans, older retired people, or even younger people willing to donate time become caretakers of wild cat colonies. Using live traps bated with food, they capture cats and bring them in to be vaccinated, neutered and ear tipped. During the neutering process males have the tip of their left ear surgically removed to identify them as having been neutered. Females have the right ear tipped because it has been said that, "Females are always right."

Our community had a few informally organized older single women who each volunteered to care for a feral colony. It gave them a purpose in their retirement years and they became dedicated caregivers. If a new cat showed up without a tipped ear they patiently trapped cats until they finally caught the newcomer to be brought in for a veterinary *take out party.*

Unfortunately, a veterinary hospital always has odors: the obvious dark heavy smell of dog and cat pee and poop, the biting eye-watering fumes of antiseptics and cleaning agents, wisps of alcohol, and occasional wafts of anesthetic gasses. The ceiling exhaust fans draw out the unpleasantness and pull in fresh clean air from the opposite end of the clinic. It is tougher in the winter when you tried to conserve heat. Sadly, the kennel room and recovery area, if occupied, typically have an obvious animal fragrance.

Some Mondays could be even worse. This was the day the TNT cats were brought in. Nobody knew when a cat might be captured and brought in. It was entirely up to the cat and I think it's safe to say that cats have a mind of their own and are unpredictable.

Do you know anybody who eats canned mackerel? I don't, but cats can't resist it. It's nutritious, oily, disgusting looking, and VERY smelly. I could enter the *staff only* door and know there was a wild cat awaiting my attention. You couldn't get the procedure done fast enough if only to clean the wild trap and dispose of the smell of the uneaten stinky mackerel.

Mildred was one of our *ladies*. She was old, tiny, and bent under the weight of her years. She still drove her car but had to peer from under the large steering wheel of her old Buick *boat*. She faithfully visited her colony every day taking food and water and checking for newcomers. She was waiting for me.

"Doctor, I've been out trying to catch thus huge orange tom cat for weeks and I finally got him. He's been terrorizing and beating up all the other males and needs a personality adjustment. I can't wait to have you castrate him," she said with a knowing smile.

We said, "Come back at the end of the day to pick him up and you can release him back to the colony. He'll be a changed man."

Mr. Tom was waiting for us in the wild trap in the kennel room. The first thing we did was turn the exhaust fan on high in spite of the outside freezing temperatures. Understandably, wild cats, when trapped, become frantic. The fragrance of oily fish, Tom cat urine, and cat poop greeted us. I told my assistant jokingly, "I'll fire up the chain saw while you bring in the cat."

Mary returned as far as the door into the treatment area when Mr. Tom exploded and escaped her grasp. We had assumed his bowel and bladder were empty but were we ever wrong. Mr. Tom proceeded to ricochet around the room bouncing off the walls and skidding across the counters and floor. He left a putrid stream of brown and yellow in his wake and finally collapsed panting in the corner. Mary brought me the salmon net and I proceeded to attempt to net my *fish*. As I approached, he launched himself straight for my head. Like a lacrosse player I was ready to catch the flying projectile, but fortunately, the floor was slippery and he spun out and only reached as far and as high as my left foot. And the battle was on. I was too occupied to create a mental picture of the scene but later Mary was gleefully more than willing to fill in the details to the rest of the staff.

Mr. Tom attacked my foot before I could fend him off. His hind claws were viciously raking my lower leg which was fortunately protected by my Levi's and the leather uppers of my western boot. His front claws were hugging my leg in a most unfriendly fashion. His teeth were tearing frantically through my Levi's trying to kill the pull tap of the boot top. It was said that I stood there on one leg trying desperately to shake him off the other; kind of like discovering you just stepped in some fresh doo-doo, which I probably had. Mary calmly caught my leg, with Mr. Tom attached, in the salmon net. It was just like a YouTube scene from ***When Wild Animals Attack.***

Eventually, we got him under control, injected an anesthetic under the skin (usually given IV), and sent him to temporary dream land. There was a definite inclination that the chain saw would have been an appropriate surgical instrument to complete the job.

We had to vaccinate my boots for distemper and rabies and were pleased to report that they survived their health scare. I still have both feet intact but the Levi's did retain a permanent scar however. Mr. Tom was reportedly peacefully ruling over his abandoned building empire and became a perfect example of a retired former tom cat.

# HERCULES

Is there anything cuter than a baby goat? They appear magically in the spring just as the weather changes and the first dandelions are jumping out of your lawn and the crocuses explode from your flower beds. They don't have legs but rather four pogo sticks that can propel them forward, upwards, sideways, and backwards seemingly simultaneously. Kids have a naïve curiosity and fearlessness that gets them into all sorts of mischief and compromising circumstances. They can climb anything, and go anywhere they can insert their compact little bodies. Their child like cry seems to trigger the maternal instinct of humans who are attracted to these captivating little animals like moths to light.

Is there anything more patient and calming than a mama goat? They can stand quietly while being assaulted from behind by their hungry kids. They don't get rattled by the little problems in life and seem content just to enjoy the moment. Their breath smells like fresh green salad or fresh mown hay when they snort or sniff you in the face. They always seem happy to see you and greet you with a bleat that seems to be a combination of a question, a demand, and a complaint. It's difficult to be grumpy in the presence of a happy curious doe.

And lastly, is there anything more obnoxious than a billy goat? They stomp around the barnyard like a king surveying his empire. Few animals will challenge them, realizing a confrontation could result in a serious head butting. It's like talking to a tree; you're not going to change its mind. They are really only good for one thing: helping to make baby goats. During the breeding season, they become strangely irresistible to female goats. They accomplish this through the odor and pheromones of the scent gland secretion produced near their horns and also their urine which they delightfully spray all over their bellies, beards, and legs. Everybody needs one for a house guest. Truly and unimaginably irresistible! If you are a lady goat in season.

Hercules was such a goat. He was a truly obnoxious, very stinky, and very large Saanen buck. He weighed at least 250 pounds. I suspect he got his name because he was so exceptionally strong (smelling?). He had a shelf full of ribbons from county fairs and expositions and also had countless progeny scattered through his empire. He lived on a small hobby farm in a barn (downwind from his owner's house) with a pasture. Gerald was an architect and Hercules was his pride and joy. Owners of does (female goats) would visit Hercules' farm in the fall and rub a rag over the oily stinky secretions on the side of Hercules face. These rags were put in Ziploc bags and delivered home to be examined by the does. If they waged their tails in a characteristic ecstatic fashion the owner then knew it was time for the doe to have an up-close-and-personal encounter with Hercules. He didn't even have to chase after ladies, for they were deposited on his threshold by special delivery.

Everyone has heard stories or seen pictures, showing how owners' faces can resemble those of their pets. I'm afraid Gerald took a certain amount of good-natured ribbing because he sported a graying full goatee and liked to be comfortable wearing an old raggedy knit sweater. At least he was fastidious about his personal hygiene and was able to go to his office not smelling like an old billy goat. Nevertheless, friends sometimes joked, "It's hard to tell which one is the old goat."

One spring, Hercules' propensity for being the barnyard bully finally landed him in deep doo-doo. Gerald had an old retired bay mare named Sally and when Hercules was bored he liked to ram her in the butt with his (fortunately hornless) head. She was usually amazingly tolerant but one day she finally had enough and blasted him with both barrels. Gerald happened to be looking out his kitchen window to see her whirl and kick Hercules. She caught him broadside and on the back end and sent him sailing through the air. He finally landed and lay there for a minute astonished and stunned. He got up determinedly a minute later only to discover his left rear leg was dangling at a disturbing angle.

That's why on that warm spring afternoon I got a phone call from Gerald. He said, "I think Hercules pushed his luck too far. Sally finally had her fill and kicked him and I think his leg is broken." I got in my truck and followed the winding dirt road through second-growth timber to Gerald's secluded little hobby farm. I made sure I had an extra pair of coveralls in the back because I knew I wouldn't be welcome back at the office smelling like an old billy goat. It didn't take long to determine that Hercules indeed had a broken left femur.

I said, "It looks like Hercules breeding days are over. It doesn't seem to make sense to put a lot of money into fixing up an old billy goat."

Gerald said, "We've been bachelor buddies far too long for me just to give up on him. Let's see if we can put him back together again."

The next morning, we scrubbed and sterilized our large indoor dog run and got the orthopedic surgery packs ready. Gerald brought Hercules in screaming his indignation about being manhandled. Perhaps he feared we might do more than just fix his leg. Some good veterinary downers quickly relaxed him and made him much more agreeable and manageable. He soon looked pretty silly on the surgery table with a shaved naked hind leg and with his head hanging over the end with a bucket beneath to catch the drool.

We incised the skin over his left thigh and probing through the heavy muscles located the broken bones. We drove a stainless-steel rod from the hip area down through the hollow bone marrow cavity of the femur and into the lower fragment towards his knee. Someone said, "I wonder what goat shish-kabob taste like?"

Someone else commented, "I expect it would make pretty good fondue as well." Using flexible stainless-steel wire, we laced and lashed the other small fragments back into their proper position like a somewhat gory jigsaw puzzle. Three rows of sutures, pain medication, some anti-inflammatories, and some post-surgical antibiotics and Hercules was good to go. I think we all gave silent mental sighs of relief when Gerald suggested that he take Hercules home while he was still sedated. At least that way he would be able to watch him through the night and we would be deprived of the pleasure of his odor. We had wisely chosen to use disposable surgical drapes but even after several scrubbings with strong bleach the area still smelled like old billy goat.

About eight weeks later I took a leisurely drive out to Gerald's farm and using light sedation pulled the 18 inch stainless steel rod out of Hercules leg. That fall in early October I got a phone call from Gerald. He said, "I thought you might like to know that Hercules had his first lady visitor this morning." You could almost hear the smile in his voice when he added, "They seemed to get along well."

Eventually I sold that practice to move my family to another city offering a better school system. I had the opportunity to go back and visit my old staff and couldn't help but smile when I detected the faint cloying odor of Hercules in that dog run.

# DOC

I don't know how he got his name, but somehow it seemed to fit. He was just Doc, a standard black and tan dachshund. Old style, full sized dachshunds were bred in Germany as long ago as the 16th century to smell, chase, and dig out badgers or other burrowing animals. They are quick, smart, and independent. They may bark excessively, are very loyal, and are suspicious of strangers. Fortunately they are too short to pee on your knees. This pretty much described Doc.

Doc had been the joy of their life. The nest had long since been empty, so he took them for walks and protected the house and premises from cats and other dangerous intruders, from his outpost on the sill of their front window. He also collected travel stickers to be posted on the back of their camper. He did, however, suffer from the Napoleonic complex being of short stature.

Doc's owners had retired from an auto repair shop business (Dad wrenched and Mom penciled) but they remained active in the community in volunteer capacities. I saw Doc initially for neutering and then once or twice each year for routine matters. I don't think he ever forgave me for that first major insult to his manhood. I don't think I ever survived unbitten from an office visit with him. He was quick; too quick for me, in fact. It seemed unfair to muzzle an 18-lb. dog but it would have been the more prudent thing to do. He never drew blood but always left me with minor bruises or tender spots.

Dachshunds are essentially dwarfs. Their long bones never complete their growth leaving a fairly normal torso but short legs. Unfortunately, their back is not quite normal with the intervertebral discs tending to calcify early. Consequently, these discs can herniate, sadly damaging the spinal cord with partial or complete paralysis of the pelvis and hind legs. Such was Doc's luck.

Harold and Betty looked pretty grim when they brought Doc in. They were knowledgeable about the risk for doxy back issues but decided to take their chances because they liked the breed's spirit and independent personality. Doc had lost most sensation and control of his back end. He was frustrated because he could only drag his back legs behind him like a seal but was in no apparent pain. As expected he tried to nip me while I examined him. An X-Ray confirmed a slipped or herniated disc in his lower back. "You warned us about this when we discussed getting a puppy," Harold said. "What are our options?"

I listed them; "Surgery, with a positive outcome by no means assured, medical treatment requiring greatly restricted activity, or euthanasia. You can treat them at home but it is a huge amount of work and many people are overwhelmed."

"Well, we're retired and have nothing but time. The decision is a no brainier for us. Just tell us what to do," said Harold.

And so it began. Posterior paralysis dogs have little or no bowel or bladder control. The bowel sort of takes care of itself. If you push marbles in one end of a pipe they eventually start plopping out the other end. The bladder is another matter, however. It may just dribble but overfills and gets stretched out of shape leading to bladder infections. Consequently, you have to assist them to urinate 4+ times a day by gently squeezing on their belly and therefore the bladder. With a male dog, this means they pee in your hand. At least it's warm.

**Can I give you a lift?**

They got an old baby play pen and put it in the place of honor in the middle of the living room so Doc could always be part of family activities. They found an old red Radio Flyer wagon and went for walks around the neighborhood pulling the wagon with Doc propped up on his own comforter. They modified a child's car seat so he could help drive the family car. But there was little sign of improvement or recovery. We became resigned to the likelihood that Doc would never walk again. I modified a set of doggy wheels and Doc quickly learned to navigate around his neighborhood pulling his hind end in a self-propelled wheelbarrow.

Weeks passed with little change. I sometimes made courtesy home visits to check on Doc. During midwinter, Harold passed on some encouraging information. When they took Doc out to his favorite private outdoor *facilities* and supported his back end, he was starting to demonstrate some bowel and bladder control. But he still couldn't walk and continued to drag his hind legs behind. This appeared to be as good as it was going to get but at least he had control of some important body functions. He was doing well with his wheels and even retrieved tennis balls. We forgot about Doc until spring when, on a whim, I stopped by for a visit. I walked up the sidewalk to the front door and was startled to see a small black pointed nose appear in the front window. Enthusiastic barking commenced immediately. No sneaking up on this household!

I knocked on the door and Betty answered. I said, "I see you made a place for Doc at the window."

"What?" she said. "He can't get up there."

"Look!" I said. Unbelievably, Doc had managed to jump onto the couch, then to the back of the couch, and from there to the window sill.

Betty said, “We've been putting him in his wheels out of habit. He must have been getting better and we didn't even notice." From that point on, Doc showed continual improvement. Initially it was a kind of drunken wandering stagger until by mid-summer, he could even trot and had fully reclaimed his throne.

We socialized with Harold and Betty's children and occasionally went water skiing at a nearby reservoir. This was one of Doc's favorite activities: riding in the bow of the ski boat or supervising the dock. On a hot August day, I was doing a water skiing dock start. One foot has a ski and you stand on the other foot until the ski rope pulls you off the end of the dock. Doc was in his usual capacity as dock master. As I took off, I felt a sharp pain in my lower left calf. I skied anyway but when I got back to the dock someone said, "What's wrong with your leg?" There was blood and four fang marks on my lower leg. The local veterinary crime scene investigator confirmed that the bite marks matched the pattern of Doc’s canine teeth. Obviously, Doc had still never forgiven me for the irreparable damage I had done to him years before, when he was just a poor helpless puppy.

**Come on in. The water’s fine**

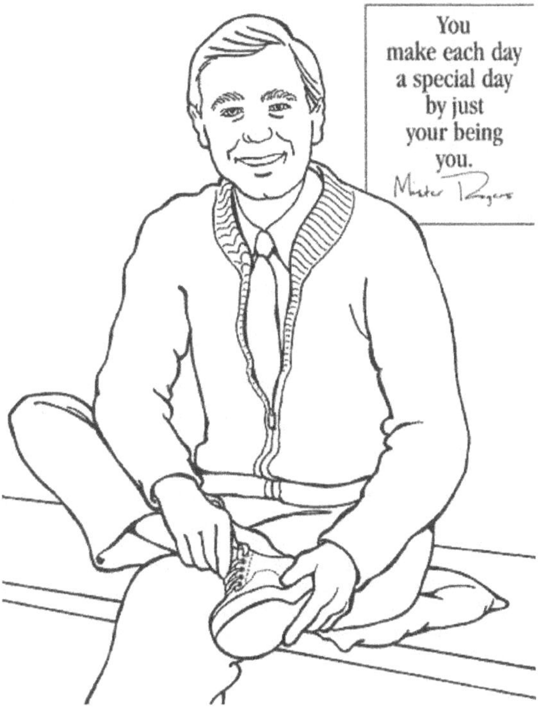


# MR. ROGER'S NEIGHBORHOOD

Who would have thought that Mr. Rogers lived right here in our neighborhood? Well, not really. But it could have been his brother. Ralph had never married and lived with his mother on the small farm his grandfather had homesteaded. He was a primary level school teacher in a nearby large city where he had an apartment, but he commuted to the farm on Fridays for the weekend. He was the perfect teacher for 6 to 12-year-old children: somehow able to be kind and compassionate but at the same time able to command respect and maintain control of the classroom. He was always eager to pass along happy anecdotes about his students and was the kind of teacher I would want for my own child. I occasionally saw him in his teacher's uniform: penny loafers, white shirt, and tie topped off with a knit cardigan sweater. He had a gentle smile, kind eyes, was soft spoken, and was always politely insisting on calling me *Doctor*.

Because he was only home for weekends, I usually saw him on Saturdays. The county road to the farm passed through meadows full of wild flowers and butterflies, heavy timber, and over quiet streams shaded by overhanging branches. The farm had become pretty run down after his father's death because Ralph didn't have much time for maintenance. He kept the farm going mainly for his mother's sake, and, in fact, it probably kept her alive giving her a purpose in life. There were some cows, a few sheep, some old retired horses, too many cats, and a small pack of dogs.

Decisions were always based on what was best for the animals but family planning was not part of the equation. This explained the large cat population but also the shortage of barnyard rodents. Old animals were allowed to quietly live out their lives up to the point where humane euthanization was appropriate. Horses that had outlived their usefulness and cows no longer capable of reproducing got all the grass they could eat in the summer and shelter with a manger full of meadow hay in the winter.

And then there were the dogs. I think the pack originated with a small stray border collie cross bitch found shivering on the porch during an especially nasty winter cold spell. Inevitably, she was soon relocated to a blanket alongside the wood stove with a bowl of warm milk and scrambled eggs. She showed her unending gratitude two weeks later by presenting Ralph and his mother with eight squeaky black and white puppies. Come springtime seven of them found homes with neighbors and Safeway patrons but one little male stayed home to keep Blackie, as she came to be known, company. Sadly, this pattern repeated itself annually because Ralph couldn't bear the thought of having his dogs neutered. Additionally, appropriate genetic decisions were not factored in. Breeding closely related animals often results in perpetrating genetic defects and this was the case with Ralph's pack. A few years and dog generations later, a litter was eventually delivered with three normal puppies, two stillborn, one with a flattened defective chest cavity, and one with microphthalmia (very small undeveloped non-seeing eyes).

I finally convinced Ralph to neuter his pack which now numbered six but he insisted on keeping the blind puppy, saying, "We'll just keep her in the kitchen." Puppies are born blind and deaf but have an acute sense of smell from birth. This is how they find their way to a nipple. At 7 – 10 days the ear canals open and adult ear shape starts to form. The puppies soon recognize their mother's voice and even that of their litter mates. At 10 – 14 days their eyes open and they develop blurry vision. By 3 months their vision clears as they begin exploring outside the nest area. It's fun to watch a litter go through these developmental stages and Ralph kept me informed as to *Girl's* progress.

I lost track of the *family farm* until a late spring morning. The pussy willows and daffodils were done, the Alder leaves had filled out, and Big Creek slid quietly between its banks when I was called out to assist with a calving problem. After I had successfully delivered a live calf, I looked around to see an audience of seven dogs closely watching my every move. It was a good thing I hadn't made any mistakes. The half-grown blind puppy was right there *watching* in the thick of it. Ralph explained, "When the weather warmed, I let her out into the fenced yard. One day I came back to the house for lunch and she was missing. I meant to go looking for her after eating but I looked out the window to see the whole pack coming in from the fields with Girl stumbling right along behind. After that, I tried to keep her in the yard but she cried and barked so much I finally relented and let her go with the rest of the dogs."

He explained, that at first, he walked with the pack to be Girl's seeing eye person but realized that she was quickly learning to use her nose and ears to travel with the other dogs. "She didn't need me." The pack followed the same familiar route around the pasture margins, across ditches, and through wild rose thickets sometimes three times a day. They caught rodents, flushed birds, and even ran down the occasional Cottontail rabbit. Having herding ancestry, they paused to remind the sheep who was in charge and to keep the flock's ranks closed tight.

Some things I observed first hand. There were some panel gates to negotiate where the dogs had to dodge around the end of the gate to get through. Somehow Girl always managed to stop just before crashing head first into the gate and always knew which way to turn to find the dog passage hole. I once saw her catch a vole by leaping into the air like a coyote and trapping the vole under her paws. The pack took care of her. The neighborhood hunting/inspection routine involved crossing a county road and the dogs seemed to stop, look, and even wait in the ditch until an oncoming car had passed by. If you drove by on the county road and saw the pack out in the pasture, you would never realize that there was a totally blind dog in their midst. Initially, Girl barked a warning when I got out of my truck but soon learned perhaps by the sound of my truck and the smell of my coveralls that I was a friend allowed on the farm. She liked to tag along close behind me occasionally brushing my pantleg. If she became disoriented she would stop with her nose in the air to catch smells drifting on the breeze. It seemed that her ears never stopped moving and even changed direction and shape to catch the sounds of her surroundings. Taking her cues from the other dogs she even helped with the herding when it was time to move the stock to a new pasture.

Ralph loved his classroom and taught well beyond the usual retirement age. Finally, he reluctantly turned his classroom over to the new teacher and resigned himself to becoming a full-time gentleman farmer. The timing was fortuitous for his mother was beginning to fail as she approached her late 80's and she was less able to help with the animals. Girl was also getting old and was happy to be assigned the position of *house dog* to keep *Mother* company. She still helped Ralph with morning chores and still occasionally traveled with the pack but spent the rest of her time helping Mother.

More green springs and colorful falls passed and the size of the farm menagerie gradually diminished. The happy rural routine continued until one fall morning when Mother didn't wake up. When Ralph opened the bedroom door, he found her with Girl sitting beside the bed listening intently. Later that winter, Ralph called to say that Girl could not be roused that morning when he found her curled up comfortably on her rug bedside the wood stove. "When she no longer had a job to do, she faded fast after Mother passed."

Even gentle Ralph is gone. The animals were mostly given to neighbors and the buildings have deteriorated beyond saving.

The pastures are overgrown with young evergreens and alders where deer, elk, and cottontails have replaced the livestock. Big Creek still passes silently between its grassy banks. But the memory of Girl lingers on.

# BEDTIME STORY

The Jones were timothy hay producers and the family had been in the valley for at least three generations and even before statehood. They had acquired some of their property through homesteading and the rest by buying out neighbors who hadn't survived the hard times. Great grandpa had dry land farmed with horses and even kept six or eight milk cows around to send milk into the local Kittitas County Dairyman's Association creamery. Great grandma still churned butter and any leftover dairy product was used to *slop the pigs*. She had a quilting frame in the corner of her parlor and sold excess free-range eggs from her mailbox at the end of the lane. In keeping with the family's tradition of frugality and diversification, Mr. Jones kept a small herd of beef cattle to consume the lower quality hay that could not be sold through local hay dealers, and to graze the fields too rocky to produce hay. The boys were not so frugal and could have managed quite well without the cattle. "Just when we think we're getting caught up, Dad always finds something to do to the cows: vaccinate, delouse, fix broken fence, and pregnancy checking." As long as Mr. Jones was alive, cattle would be part of the family operation. At least there were three of them to split up the herdsmanship responsibilities.

Late winter evokes memories for cattleman and large animal veterinarians. There is family sledding with the blast of frigid snow in your face, the shivery chill of sliding between cold sheets, the heavy oily smells of a warm farm shop, the kitchen aroma of fresh baked bread and goodies from the oven, feeding the cows as the steam rises off their backs, the satisfaction of a freshly snowplowed drive and barnyard, feeling the glow on your face from the wood fire, and hot chocolate or coffee maybe with a little nip added. And then, there is the beginning of calving season: middle of the night calls, permanently chapped cracked hands, rolling around in the mud with boots full of ice water, but also the satisfaction of seeing a new life enter the world. This time of long winter nights can also be a time of short days and little rest for a cattle rancher and livestock veterinarian. Somehow my mind and body had learned to activate and answer the phone semi-consciously even before the first ring had stopped. My wife, beside me, managed to blissfully sleep right through it all, or at least did a great job of job of faking it. It was what I called a groaner. You *groaned*, got out of bed, pulled on your coveralls and crawled behind the wheel of your truck.

This was one of those nights. I don't know what time it was; somewhere around zero dark thirty. I picked up the phone and mumbled incoherently into it. It was the younger Jones boy who said, "We've got a calving problem. Can you come out? It took us an hour to get her out of the calving pasture up to the barn, but we are ready and waiting for you." I found yesterday's coveralls still standing dirty and upright in the corner of laundry room, and pulled them on over my long underwear. It was about 10° and the snow complained and squeaked under the tires as the truck idled down the driveway. I luckily remembered to turn on my headlights before I hit the county road. The Jones barn dated back to the horse era and even had a stanchion to secure a cow for milking. It had been fully modernized with a few dusty cobweb covered hanging electric lightbulbs and gravity fed spring water for the water trough.

They had a bucket of hot water steaming but quickly chilling inside the door. It took us another half hour to drive the cow from the barnyard into the barn where we finally captured her inside a 30 foot pen. By then she was on the flight. Frantic, exhausted, all her survival instinct kicked into hyperdrive; she was ready to take on the world. Still half awake and bleary eyed, I climbed over the fence and stepped into the straw filled pen. I heard a shout and looked up to see a wild eyed crazed cow charging me. I scrambled back and managed to reach the top rail of the fence only to get hammered in the butt by the rock-hard head of a killer cow. Fortunately, she had no horns but lifted me right up over the top of the fence to land unharmed on my feet like a cowboy gymnast on the other side. There was a derisory cheer from the audience and someone said, "I score that an 8.6."

The Jones were farmers, not cowboys, so they were more than content to watch me while I lured the cow into the stanchion head catch using myself as bait. The overall situation didn't look very promising. The exhausted cow stank and bellowed frantically as she fought desperately to escape the head catch. Stripping down to my tee shirt, I plunged my arm into that now frigid bucket of water. I handed her tail, which had frozen bricks of manure on the end, to one of the boys to hold so I wouldn't get a concussion or be beat to death. Soaping up my arm and dodging flying hind feet, I reached into the birth canal where it was at least warm. It didn't take long to discover that the calf was in a head back presentation. It was trying to come out chest and shoulder first with the head and neck folded back. You have to push everything back into the uterus to provide space to capture the head. Meanwhile the cow was putting all her effort into delivering the calf and thus fighting your effort to push it back in. Based on the odor, the cow's fatigue, and the prolonged time in labor, we all knew that the calf would be delivered dead. Head snare, leg chains, and calf puller eventually delivered the limp body to the straw covered floor. "Well, at least that's over," said Mr. Jones.

Out of habit I put my hand on the calf's chest searching for a heartbeat to be certain that it was in fact dead. To my astonishment, I felt a faint flutter, like a butterfly's wings on your fingertips. Thump on the chest, extend the neck, pull on the tongue, tickle the nostrils with a straw or the tip of your little finger; and the calf sucked in a desperate gasp of air. We were astounded. "Do you believe in miracles?" The cow had been in labor for 12 hours, and beyond all reason, had managed to deliver a live calf. I reexamined the birth canal for damage, checked the cow's udder for milk and rubbed fetal fluids all over her face and muzzle to encourage maternal instincts. Finally, we released the head catch to free the cow and she stood there obliviously panting for the about a minute. I was climbing back up over the fence with my bucket and equipment when the cow realized she was free, saw me, and again tried to escort me from her universe. I escaped unharmed but the enraged cow circled the pen looking for someone to kill and an escape route, stepped on her newborn calf, and killed it.

By then it was daylight and time for me to go to my office and start morning surgeries.

# NO HITCHHIKING ALLOWED

My receptionist said," A lady just walked in the front door, put this kitten on the counter, smiled sweetly, turned around, and walked out. I have no idea who she was. What should I do with the kitten?" I was in the middle of a surgery, and it was a decision way above my pay grade. I grumbled, " Put it in a kennel and I'll deal with it later." When *later* came it was late Friday evening and the animal shelter wouldn't open again until Monday morning.

So, the orange tabby kitten went to work practicing its magic arts on us. First of all, it was just too damn cute. Then it got underfoot, rubbed against our legs, purred, bounced around chasing cotton balls and laser lights on the floor, ate, pooped in a litter box, slept, and did other hugely annoying things. We just couldn't take any more *punishment* so when Monday morning rolled around nobody had the heart to take it to the animal shelter.

Well, you can guess the kitten's final disposition. My wife, who often assisted me, came in and saw it and said, “We'll just take it home." Fortunately for me, our youngest daughter saw it and decided that she could take it home. However, there proved to be some level of incompatibility with two large bouncy dogs. So, the kitten got handed off to the oldest daughter who took it home. By then the cute little yellow tabby kitten had turned into a large yellow tabby cat who proceeded to squabble with the oldest daughter's retired elderly cat.

So off he went to the father-in-law's farm where he quickly took over the job of guarding and protecting the cattle barn. He terrorized the rats, mice, and starlings that liked to nest in the eaves. One of his favorite sleeping places was in the young Angus bull's grain feeder trough and he seemed to have no objections when the young bulls left him dripping wet with drool by constantly licking him. However, the father-in-law sold the cattle and moved away from the farm. The renters of the farmhouse didn't want a large yellow tabby cat hanging around so he got evicted. And guess where he wound up. Again!

Turns out it was a great arrangement for both of us. We put him in our horse barn where he guarded the premises and put the rodents under 24-hour lock down. That's when he finally got a permanent name: Barney. He liked to hang around the house on occasion in hopes that he might be let in but eventually became quite content to hang out in the barn where he kept the horses company. It also protected him from becoming a coyote's main course. On sunny days, he would lie down in the horse stall area, often within inches of their feet. They seemed to know he was there and did a careful shuffling two-step to avoid squashing him.

Barney has an innate uncanny ability to read body language. My Border Collie or my son's Standard Poodles can come racing up and he just stands his ground and then just rubs against them and sniffs noses. With strange dogs, he sometimes dashes for safety but other times stands his ground and dares them to come within striking distance. I guess he reads me also because when he is hungry he walks slowly in front of me making me slow down or stumble over him. When he knows he has my attention, he dashes over to his food dish and meows until he gets fed. He often shows his appreciation by leaving gifts of vole livers or tails on the front porch doormat.

One spring day, I planned to haul hay to the west side of the mountains for a friend who boarded horses. The hay had been compressed and wrapped in plastic one-ton packages for export to Asia. I put two of these in the back of my truck and parked in my driveway for a few minutes for a snack before starting the trip. I stopped at a nearby freeway exit to get fuel and then drove off. 75 miles later I pulled over at an exit to talk on my cell phone and feeling sleepy decided to take a 10-minute nap. West Side traffic was busy so it was stop and go and it took almost three and a half hours to reach my destination.

I arranged to meet my friend at a Chinese restaurant for lunch. We had our egg flower soup and pork chow mein and sat around for half an hour just chatting. As I walked out to get back into my truck I heard a strange sound. I stopped to listen carefully and realized it was a faint plaintive meow coming from the back of my truck. I looked into the box and my heart stopped. There was Barney crouched exposed and shivering on the cold steel deck next to the plastic wrapped hay packages. It seemed like a full minute before I could catch my breath and sense that my heart had started beating again. There had been no place to hide. He was a curious cat and must have jumped up into my truck to investigate when the truck was parked in my driveway. Why he had not run away or attempted to escape sometime during the trip baffles me to this day. Fearing that he would be frightened and trying to escape now, I very carefully gathered him up to put him in the cab of the truck. He leaped up on my chest and wrapped his front legs tightly around my neck. Once we were in the cab I sat there for five minutes thinking about what could have happened. He could have jumped out anywhere and I could only have assumed he had disappeared from the barn at home. There are, of course, many stories about dogs and cats that have traveled hundreds of miles to return home and be reunited with their caregivers. Barney had been exceedingly lucky.

He got to spend the rest of the weekend getting lots of attention in a large kennel kept in my friend's house. He seemed especially pleased when two days later I returned him to his own kingdom in the horse barn. He continued to explore the parked truck and horse trailer on occasion but always made a rapid exit whenever the engine started. I have also learned to look for stowaways and hitchhikers ever since.

About two months after this incident a gray half-grown tom cat showed up in my barn. When I gently tried to persuade him to establish residence elsewhere, he demurred and just climbed up on top of the hay pile and calmly looked down at me. Fortunately, the new cat, who came to be known as Lucky, was sociable and would wait patiently until Barney had his fill of cat food and then would quietly move in to get his share. Since he wouldn't leave and didn't seem to have a home elsewhere, I finally took him in to my office and vaccinated and neutered him. He kept his distance from me for a few days after that before finally deciding that perhaps I wasn't so bad after all. I don't understand why he temporarily became so standoffish. So now we had a two-cat barn.

However, as often seems to be the case when a cat is neutered, about two months later he disappeared. I despaired thinking that perhaps a coyote had finally got him but then he reappeared for a few days. That pattern continued and he would come and go but spend most of his time elsewhere. One day I stopped in to talk with my neighbor Bob as he was barbecuing on his porch. He offered me a beer and we sat chatting.

I asked him, "You didn't happen to see a young gray cat around did you?"

He said, "You mean that one over there?" I looked and there was Lucky on the other end of the porch washing his face, having just finished a dinner of cat kibble garnished with hamburger drippings. I had to laugh! Lucky was playing both ends against the middle. Instead of having two wives, he had two well-trained providers. Bob said, "I wondered if there was a story behind this nice cat who showed up on my doorstep, who was already missing his *huevos*."

About a month later I decided to go on a trail ride with my horses. I caught the horses, brushed them, and loaded them into the horse trailer. Barney and Lucky often watched these proceedings. After a half hour drive I got to the trailhead and opened the back of the trailer to unload the horses. There was something strange on the floor down by their feet. I looked more closely to discover that Lucky was crouched there almost hugging the right front foot of my mare. Again, I carefully gathered up a freeloading stowaway hitchhiker and put him in the cab of my truck. I went on my trail ride and stopped at Bob's house on the way home to return his/our cat. Bob smiled and said, "Are you trying to steal my cat?"

There must be something about my wanderlust and need for adventure that appealed to these cats and they therefore thought it would be fun to come along and keep me company. Fortunately, they were smart enough or lucky enough to not get lost in the process. Barny still resides in my barn and meows demandingly whenever I open the door. Lucky still stops in for a visit once or twice a month and I see him perched on top of the haystack observing the goings-on. I can imagine Barney and Lucky talking about the weather, their favorite new flavor of cat food, and bragging about their mouse catching skills.

Like the words from the Crosby, Stills, and Nash song *Our House: With two cats in the yard.* My song lyrics would be, *My barn is a very, very, very, nice barn. With two cats by the door and everything is easy.* My adventuresome cats have been off to see the wonderful wide world but have now decided to settle in and be homebodies. I put a sign on the back window of my truck:

**NO HITCHHIKERS!**

**Anneke**

# THE WELDED COW

"Doctor, would you please come out and look at my heifer? You don't know me but this is Lars Bossen over in Matsqui." You could hear the worry in his voice.

I asked, "What's wrong Lars?"

"She's got a broken back leg," was the answer. "My regular vet looked at her and said to just shoot her. I called two other doctors and they wouldn't even come out when I told them what was wrong. I paid a lot of money just to get her blood lines. I can't just let her go. She's only been on the farm for three weeks and we haven't even named her yet. It's like wrecking your brand-new car."

Lars was the rather portly sire of a large family of four sons and a daughter in British Columbia, Canada. They owned a herd of well-managed purebred Holstein Friesian dairy cows. The Bossen Dairy ran like a Swiss clock with each person fulfilling his role to make things run efficiently. Lars was the pendulum that kept everything in time. They took great pride in their high-producing purebred cows and were always on the lookout for bloodlines that would improve the herd quality. They not only produced milk but sold breeding bulls and surplus heifers as well.

That spring they had purchased a purebred heifer from eastern Saskatchewan for the unheard-of price of $5,000. They had turned her out with the older cows onto the lush spring grass waiting for her to come into heat so she could be bred. When a cow is in season (in heat) other cows mount her thus alerting the bull that his services are desired. (In modern dairy management, most cows are artificially inseminated. The *bull* hides in a tank of liquid nitrogen). A live bull is only kept for backup.) This heifer had been mounted by a large older cow and been knocked down. In the process, her right rear leg was broken.

I squeezed in time during my lunch break to drive down their tree lined lane. A cold rain was falling so hard it bounced off the pavement and the wipers struggled to keep up. At least the barn was warm with 150 furnaces running; and burping and passing gas. It was a carefully maintained old wooden flat barn where the cows walk into their own personal stanchion and you lock a catch on their neck when they put their heads into the trough to get grain.

She stood there trembling and panting on three legs. It looked pretty bad. The tibia was broken about 4 inches above the hock, equivalent to just above a human ankle. The lower part of her leg just dangled there grotesquely. It would be bad enough if it were a dog or cat but this puppy weighed 800lbs. I said, "Wow!" I flopped down on a bale of straw to think. "There are two techniques we use on pets but neither is strong enough for her."

Lars said, "I'm pretty desperate. Could you at least try?"

Thinking out loud I said, "Maybe if I combined both techniques together it might work but where would I get materials strong enough?"

"How about Ernie's Welding Shop?" Lars asked.

Unconsciously chewing on a carefully selected long straw I said, "I'll make some calls and be over at the end of the day".

"We'll be waiting, and Mum will have a hot meal for you," Lars replied.

"I don't want to make any bold promises but I'll give it my best effort," I said.

"That's all I can ask," said Lars.

Ernie not only had what I needed but asked if he could help. "We go way back. I went to high school with Lars," he said. He showed up at 6 p.m. with his portable welder, acetylene cutting torch, pipe cutters, grinder, 1-inch steel pipe, 5/16-inch stainless steel rod, four rolls of duct tape, and 2 six packs of Kokanee Beer.

So, with the whole family watching and helping when they could, we welded the heifer back together. Part of my apparatus was a modified giant Kirchner external pin fixation assembly. It's not quite as complicated as it sounds. Imagine driving sharpened stainless-steel rods like arrows parallel to the ground through the broken tibia bone three above and three below the fracture site. Then we drilled six matching holes in each of two steel straps to slide over the pins on each side of the leg like building a ladder which incorporated the broken bones. Trickling garden hose water on the site kept it cool during the welding and prevented making Holstein shish kabob. This device stabilized the fracture but wouldn't be able to stand up to full weight bearing.

Now using the pipe, we built a giant Thomas splint. Imagine putting the leg through a large padded steel donut ring all the way up to the hip. Then attach rods to the front and back of the ring which loop down and connect at the bottom below the hooves. The rods are longer than the leg so they transfer weight from the pelvis down to the ground when the animal stands. Now weld the whole Rube Goldberg device together.

In an hour, the sedative wore off and all six of us heaved together and lifted her to her feet. Amazingly, 20 minutes later she hobbled over to the manger in her stall and began eating. "Wow," I said again. "Amazing! Now it's up to her."

Timing it perfectly Mrs. Bossen, wearing an apron, stuck her head through the barn door and hollered," Soups on!" We scrubbed off in the mud room and the nine of us sat down in the warm farm kitchen to a feast of meat and potatoes and bread just out of the oven. Hot apple pie and ice cream was the perfect finale. We were pretty hungry since it was after midnight. I had no idea we had been working for six hours.

Not every animal is a cooperative patient but Anneke, as the Bossens came to call her, was perfect. After a few days of being assisted, she mastered the technique of standing up on her own. Lying down was a little trickier because if she lay on the wrong side the splint made it impossible for her to get up and she had to be rolled over. She soon learned to only lie down on her left side. We put her in in the maternity pen where she soon became the big sister to all the newborn baby calves.

Healing seem to be progressing nicely but after 6 weeks the donut began rubbing badly against the skin of her flank. It was obvious that that part of the apparatus had to be removed so using the acetylene cutting torch we quickly cut it off. Hot sparks ignited the straw in her stall but the Bossen fire crew was ready with a garden hose to keep the barn from burning down.

We held our breath for the next few days worrying that the remaining apparatus would not be sufficient. To our immense relief the device held and Anneke was soon walking around almost normally. The sores on her flank healed and she began to look like an ordinary heifer except she still had the pins and plates attached through and to her lower leg.

3 weeks later, using heavy bolt cutters, we cut off the six pins and pulled them out of her leg. It was weird to shine a flashlight on her leg and see the light pass right on through the holes. Again, she healed quickly and had almost stopped limping by that time. In a few weeks, they turned her out with the rest of the herd but this time carefully isolated her when she came in heat.

About that time my family's personal life took a major change. We loved the outdoor environment of British Columbia and my veterinary practice was very successful but it was not the educational environment in which I wanted to raise my son. Therefore, we returned back to my home town in Washington State (just in time to get trapped in Mount St. Helens ash) and I lost track of Anneke and the Bossons.

About a year later I got a large surprise envelope from Canada in the mail. It was from the Bosson's. Without my being aware of it, they had made a photographic record of all the events surrounding Anneke's problems. Neighbors and other dairy men had encouraged them to pass this story on to the local newspaper which printed a full-page story. Thus encouraged, they sent the story to the Canadian Dairy Journal where it was also printed. Eventually, right on schedule, Anneke was bred and delivered a 100-lb. baby heifer. The Bossens were so pleased with Anneke and her offspring that they decided to take her to the CNE (Canadian National exhibition) in Toronto, which was the largest agricultural fair in Canada. She was entered in the springer heifer division and was judged champion of her class. This arguably made her the best two-year-old cow in Canada. "Wow," I thought to myself.

I have lost track of Anneke and the Bossens through the years but I have no doubt Anneke's DNA continues in British Columbia dairy herds. I once did a veterinary literature search and could find no indication that anyone had ever welded a cow back together, before or after.

**Fluffy**

# PHONE HOME

The Rhodes were pillars of the small community. Their sundry store business had been handed down through three generation to the current family owners. "If we don't have it you probably don't need it," was the store motto. They lived about half a mile, as the crow flies, from my office on a landmark hill in the middle of the city. The house had been built before the first great war by the long since deceased great grandfather of the family. Even though it had been extensively remodeled through the years it still had a certain grandeur and class that marked the prosperous years of its origin. There were gables for each of the upstairs bedrooms, a fine brick fireplace with a walnut mantle, a large front porch with a swing, and a wide spiral staircase leading upstairs.

Fuzzy was the sole occupant of one of the upstairs bedrooms. He was a beautiful gray long haired Persian cat who enjoyed all the special privileges due the most important regal member of the household. Special food, regularly perfumed and cleaned litter box, and daily grooming were part of his daily routine. I don't think Fuzzy was ever allowed outside unsupervised. You wouldn't want him to be attacked by some wild animal such as a killer mouse or an enraged mother robin. We saw him for annual checkups and routine maintenance. He had never learned to use a scratching post so we had to perform a pedicure for his overlong claws.

Martha and her eight-year-old son brought Fuzzy in for his annual appointment. I happened to be looking out the front window when their Lincoln pulled up. I had an anxious moment when I saw Martha's son carrying Fuzzy who was struggling to escape. Fortunately, they successfully navigated the front door and I quickly retrieved a pet carrier to put Fuzzy in where he might feel more secure. We finished Fuzzy's appointment and I opened the carrier to put him back inside. Martha said, "Oh, don't bother. Bobby can carry him out to the car. He drags him all around the house like a stuffed animal so there shouldn't be any problem". I insisted but she resisted. So, Fuzzy was soon on his way out the front door back to the car. In a flash, Fuzzy wiggled, performed a beautiful Olympic backflip, and vanished around the corner of the building into the bushes. We all stood there with our mouths hanging open.

We saw him in the neighbor’s hedge row but before we could catch him he disappeared across the street and off into the neighborhood. We gathered in the parking lot not quite knowing what to say. Martha said, "I have to admit you were right. I should have known that you were more familiar with how to handle a frightened cat. It certainly wasn't your fault. I have to accept full responsibility."

I said, "I'll have one of my assistants go around and knock on a few doors and we'll see if we can make some flyers.”

It was difficult to get back into the routine to finish the afternoon's office calls. We were unsettled and couldn't help wonder what we could have done differently to prevent this disaster. About 45 minutes later the office phone rang. It was Martha. She said, "I did a little grocery shopping since we were already downtown and just now pulled into my driveway. I thought you might want to know that Fuzzy was sitting calmly on the front porch swing waiting for us." Somehow, a cat who had essentially never been outside had managed to navigate two busy streets and a mile of unfamiliar neighborhood as well as a steep rocky bank to get home. We don't know how birds navigate for their migration either. We decided he used his CPS device (cat positioning senses). Fuzzy's trip perhaps was not quite as remarkable as that of an Arctic tern but nevertheless we were greatly relieved and impressed.

# THE OLD SWIMMING HOLE

I guess wanting a little privacy at birthing time is a reasonable expectation but this Holstein cow got a little carried away. When her time came Helga just disappeared. Of course, it was right during a mid-winter snow/rain storm and in the middle of milking time so her owner Mr. Webb literally had his hands full (of cow's udders) and was unavailable for a search-and-rescue mission.

You could hear the exasperation in his voice when he rang me up (that's what some people do in Canada). "She's one of the best cows in my string and has given up to a hundred and fifty pounds of milk a day," he said. "She's also prone to milk fever." Cows get milk fever when their blood calcium levels drop too low. This comes about because the cow is starting to produce large quantities of high calcium milk and also has just produced a 100 pound calf. Calcium is necessary for proper muscle function and if the levels are too low the cow can collapse and even die of heart failure if not discovered and treated quickly.

The Webbs had a large wooded pasture with a water filled slough at the far end. It was a great place for ducks and swimming on a hot summer's day but neither had much appeal at that moment. Mr. Webb said, "I'm sorry I can't give you a hand but I think you should be able to find her back there behind the trees." So, I climbed back into the cab of my truck and slithered through the ruts to the far end of the field.

The weather was so miserable, I didn't want to get back out of the warm cab. At first, I didn't see anything, but finally, right at the edge of the water, I saw an ear twitch and a rising column of steam. Why would a cow lie down in a precarious place like the edge of a slippery bank to deliver a calf? I don't have an answer but animals sometimes do strange things like this while seeking a safe secluded place to deliver. When I walked up to her, she barely responded and didn't even twitch an ear. It was obvious that she had, in fact, collapsed with milk fever. Complicating matters, her hindquarters were submerged in about a foot of cold muddy water. I looked around desperately hoping to see a lifeguard or superhero coming to assist but it was evident that she and I were all alone in the universe with our problems.

First: keep the cow alive. You do this by administering a mixture of calcium, magnesium, and dextrose into the jugular vein in her neck. The effect of this treatment can be very dramatic and a cow that appears to be flat out and almost dead might in fact stand up after 10 minutes. However, I needed to be able to control my patient, so, I gave her only half a dose, thus keeping her in a somewhat weakened but safe condition. Underwater deliveries have had some popularity with the human species but I decided that floundering around in ice cold water was not optimal for either me, the calf, or its mother. So, with a heavy cow halter and ropes, I used my truck bumper to drag the expectant mother from the mud and up the slippery bank onto terra firma.

Next: the delivery. I was already sopping wet, cold, and muddy, so, I just sat in a puddle and put my feet against her rump to pull on the chains attached to the calf's front feet. At least the exertion warmed me up somewhat and it wasn't long until with a warm wet sploosh, a hundred-pound calf plopped out on my chest. I spent the next few minutes attending to the calf to make sure it's airways we're clear and it was breathing properly. How satisfying it is when you watch a calf first fill its lungs with air. Feeling rather smug with my success to that point, I turned around to check on the cow only to discover that she was just delivering her uterus as well. This is called a prolapsed uterus and is similar to pulling wet gloves off your hand and having them turn inside out. I'm sure anybody in the vicinity could have heard my audible grown.

So, next: reduce the prolapse. I liken it to wrestling with a 30-pound octopus trying to fight its way out of a jar while you try and push it back. Everything is washed and protected on a clean plastic tarp, the placenta is teased away and then using your thighs, belly, chest, and closed fists you gradually, carefully, force the uterus into its proper place, back inside the cow.

Next: finish treating the underlying problem. More IV calcium is administered but you carefully monitor heart rhythm and strength because if you over stimulate it in its weakened condition, it could fail. So far so good! A live calf, a successfully reduced uterine prolapse, and the cow responding nicely to her medication. However, perhaps she responded more quickly and more enthusiastically than I expected. As I was standing there monitoring her heartbeat, she suddenly swung her head and neck around trying to get on her feet and hit me like a bowling ball striking the number 10 pin. I was flipped upside down and literally landed on my head in a yet as undisturbed puddle of icier muddy water.

Just then a voice said, "Ya damn fool. Don't you know how stupid it is to go swimming alone? As long as I'm here I'll lead Helga back to the barn and you can carry the calf. I wouldn't want to get all wet and muddy." Back in the warm milking parlor, I stripped down to my undies, washed off with the warm water hose used to rinse down the cow's udders before milking, and struggled to put on a pair of oversized borrowed coveralls. A big mug of hot hard cider offered by Mrs. Webb did help to sooth my bruised frozen ego.

# IN THE BERRIES

At the very mature age of 12 years and 7 months (almost 13), I was trying to navigate the fine line between curiosity and mischief and become a teenager. I was fortunate enough to make the stabilizing acquaintance of an elder from the Yakama Nation. The stories she told of family life during her childhood were fascinating. Our family sometimes went berry picking for blackberries, black raspberries, and huckleberries during the summer. Thus, her stories of summer encampments during berry picking season were especially intriguing. She said," I'm almost the last in my family line and nobody goes berry picking or root digging anymore. There are some wonderful places I would love to visit again before I die. I have great memories of putting blankets down on the ground and then beating the bushes with sticks to knock the berries off onto the blankets. Then we would tip the blankets back and forth and the leaves and trash would stick to the blanket and the berries would roll off the other end."

"Where did you go," I asked. She smiled knowingly and gave some vague general directions to a valley up in the Teanaway area. Favorite huckleberry patches were closely held family secrets not divulged to just anyone.

She artfully dodged my question and said, "Some years were much better than others. It seems that if there had been a hard winter with deep snow followed by a relatively late spring, all the bushes bloomed at the same time and if there was enough moisture into the early summer you could have a real bumper crop. Mix the dried berries with fat and cured smoked venison or dried salmon and you got through long winters."

Years passed and she had long since passed on to her Happy Hunting Ground, where the berries were always plentiful and ripe, but I never forgot about the obscure directions to her favorite area.

It had been a hard cold winter with deep snow and spring came on slowly. It occurred to me that these were exactly the conditions that she had described so many years before. So, I loaded my horses into the trailer, opened the back door of the truck cab for the dog, and off we went to the high country. There had been a long hot spell and I figured that this might have made all the berries ripen at the same time and make for ideal picking.

We saddled up in the cool of the morning with the mist rising from the meadows. My dog bounded ahead knowing there had to be lots of things to smell and chase. The further up the trail we went and the more elevation we gained the more excited I got. There were huckleberries everywhere and they got bigger and juicier the further we traveled. Branches were so heavily laden with fruit that they were bent down with the weight. Finally, I could resist no longer so I jumped down and began stuffing my mouth. My dog wondered what I was doing so I showed her how to pluck berries off of the branches with her teeth. Finally, I loosened the cinches, tied the horses to a tree, and commenced serious picking. The berries almost fell into my bucket of their own accord. I had visions of pie, cobbler, jam, and ice cream topping.

Securing my bucket to a strap hanging around my neck, I fell into a rhythm of two handed picking and only paused briefly to admire my purple bounty. I lost all sense of time. But then a strange chill spread through the woods around me. It was starting to get dark but it was a middle of the day and there wasn't a cloud in the sky. How could this be? Here I was in the middle of the best huckleberry picking my life and it was too dark to even see what I was doing. I stumbled over to a rotten log and sat down to contemplate. Finally, laughing at myself in desperation, I said a short prayer to the great huckleberry spirit asking only that there be light enough to see to continue picking. However, I was interrupted because I had to jump up and drop my pants. I had been sitting on an ant's nest. But miraculously at the same time light began flooding back into the forest again. I filled my bucket in no time and to make sure I had enough, I spent another 15 minutes stuffing my pie hole. I sat for a few minutes to rest my tired back but when I turned around I discovered that my faithful dog had found my full pail of berries and decided was much easier to eat them from the pail then it was to pick them off the bushes. Out of respect for her brains and initiative, I did not have the heart to chastise her. They say that one of the drawbacks to having a border collie is that they are often smarter than their owner.

I hiked over to a nearby stream and took a long satisfying cold drink. I tried unsuccessfully to wash the blue off my hands and lips. Feeling satiated and happy I lay down for a short nap in the warm afternoon sun. When I woke, with a smile on my face, it was late afternoon and time to mount up and head down the valley to the lowlands.

I have often thought back to that magical afternoon in late August of 2017 and still don't understand what happened to the sun.

**TRICKY TOO**

# CARPET BAG KID

George was a prominent successful local businessman. He could be seen on our small-town sidewalks at noon walking to lunch or the Post Office wearing button-down collars, gray silk ties, a tailored business suit, and wing-tipped shoes. He often seemed a little standoffish and preoccupied but his wife Christine more than compensated. She had all the positive characteristics of a classic southern belle. She was attractive, well dressed, always cheerful, and had a kind word for everyone. She even looked good when dressed in her gardening clothes. Her southern accent could sweet talk a child out of his lollipop and leave a cowboy grinning foolishly.

But their nest was empty. George's day was filled with business activity. Christine had never had to work out of the home but had been a full-time homemaker providing their three children with a wonderful and proper upbringing. When the children had departed to start lives of their own, she became more involved with charity and community service groups. But something was missing. George finally consented to getting a pet to see if it would help fill the silent empty spaces of their home.

I recommended the Shih Tzu breed as a clean affectionate breed while admitting it was relatively high maintenance. Thus, Tricky Too became a valuable member of their household. He arrived as a black and white fuzz ball puppy tucked into the large pocket of someone's winter coat. He fit comfortably into your cupped hands or on your lap whenever he was able to convince you that he desperately needed to be picked up. Christine now had a pet to love, spoil, and play dress-up with. George initially grumbled his doubts but soon secretly came to love Tricky as much as did Christine. It didn't take Tricky long to control the household in a happy but passive-aggressive fashion. One of his favorite pastimes was chasing the dust mop. Their home had beautiful oak hardwood floors which Christine kept clean by pushing a dust mop around. She jokingly said it could be hard to distinguish the pup from the mop when Tricky tried to kill the shaggy intruder.

Christine had inherited a beautiful carpet bag from her grandmother in Georgia. Tricky discovered it in the basement one day and jumped inside. It became one of his favorite hiding places from which he could ambush his two-legged servants. Tricky loved his carpet bag cave/house/bed/couch and even preferred it to his soft pastel blue dog bed at home. He would wander anxiously around the house looking for his bag when it got sent to the dry cleaners for a semi-annual dry cleaning.

George traveled frequently with his business and once the children were gone, Christine began making trips with him. Tricky Too was Christine's surrogate child and so, of course, traveled with them. They located hotels and motels which were pet friendly and Tricky Too, being clean, quiet, and well-mannered was always welcome. On occasion, they traveled to areas where there were no dog-friendly accommodations. Using her imagination and ingenuity, Christine used Tricky's carpet bag and when they were ready to take luggage into their room, Tricky Too was hidden in the bag and carried along with the other suitcases to the night's accommodation.

This stowaway ruse worked perfectly for many years but as Tricky Too aged, he developed a heart mitral valve condition with a murmur. Medication helped and allowed for a fairly comfortable active existence but, never the less, he still had a fairly persistent moist cough. On one occasion when checking into a four-star hotel they frequented, the bellboy picked up the luggage before Christine had a chance to secure Tricky Two's carpet bag. During the elevator ride with the bellboy to the 11th floor room, a very distinct cough emanated from the carpet bag. A deafening silence reigned in the elevator. The bellboy looked startled but diplomatically said nothing and escorted them politely to their room. I suspect he didn't want to jeopardize his tip. George and Christine settled in expecting the worst and, sure enough, the hotel manager knocked on their door about 20 minutes later. He was polite but explained that the hotel did have a no-pet policy. They could stay the night but would have to pay an extra room cleaning fee.

A few months later George and Christine got a phone call from the hotel corporate offices. The gentleman on the phone said that the hotel liked to provide services for their special frequent clients and had decided to set aside a few first-floor rooms for people with pets. A refundable deposit would be required in case an 'accident' occurred.

After that, Tricky Too entered the hotel through the front door with a blue ribbon in his hair, a blue rhinestone decorated cowboy bandana around his neck, and dragging Christine behind him with his patent leather leash. The carpet bag was left in the trunk of their Lincoln.

Tricky Too died quietly in his sleep a few years later. However Tricky Three has now taken over the job of filling empty rooms with joy, killing the dust mop, and escorting his people into fancy hotels.

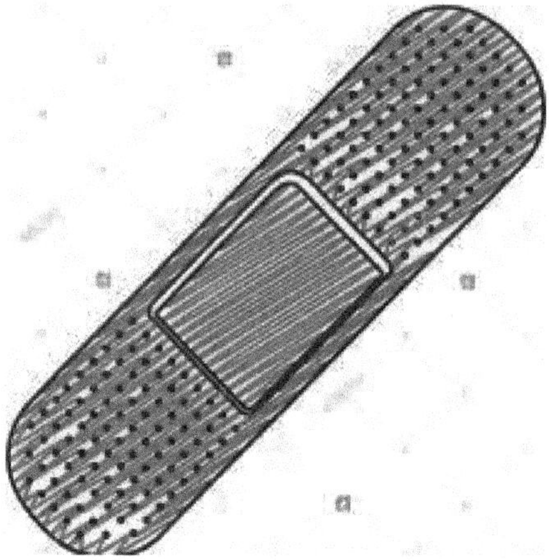

**"BAND AID"**

# BAD STUFF SOMETIMES HAPPENS (TO VETERINARIANS)

Horse anesthetics in the 1960s and 70s often did not provide a smooth recovery. Patients often struggled to get up even before they were physically capable. When I was in my senior year of veterinary school we were assisting a horse to stand after surgery. The horse staggered sideways and stepped on my foot. It became very bruised and swollen so we sneaked into the X-ray room and took a radiograph. My little toe was broken. There's not much you can do except to splint it with tape to the rest of the foot, wear soft wide shoes, and wait for it to finally heal. I still have all eleven toes.

During the late 1970s it was still customary to use a nasogastric tube (stomach tube) to get an anthelmintic (wormer) into a horse's stomach. I would walk up to a horse, smile politely, and say, "Mr. Horse! Do you see this 10-foot hose? I'm going to shove it up your nose." Needless to say, they did not always appreciate my presumptuous attitude. On one occasion the horse owner lost control of the horse's halter at the most inopportune moment. The horse reared up and struck out with a front leg hitting me on the left forearm. It hurt for several days so I took an x-ray but could not find any apparent damage. It continued to be very painful so after a week I took an identical x-ray and the hairline fracture was then quite evident in the middle of my left radius. There was no displacement so I just kept working. I still have both arms and they are relatively functional.

A 100lb logging camp guard dog was brought in having been hit by a logging truck. There was obvious damage to the pelvis, so, I sedated the dog in preparation for an x-ray. That drug could sometimes cause a dog to vomit, so, it was inappropriate to use a muzzle. When I picked up the partially awakened dog but with no control of the head or teeth, it reached up and grabbed my face. When I instinctively dropped the dog with his teeth still attached to me, my lower lip was split down towards my chin. My bookkeeper took me to the hospital where my face was repaired with 30 stitches. Then I had to go back and finish the treatment and X-ray. I still have the same face.

Veterinarians sometimes need respite from their busy schedules. We often escaped on weekend horse pack trips. We were fording a river several miles up a mountain trail in the William O. Douglas Wilderness when uncharacteristically my horse whirled and came lunging out of the water. I got tossed into the air and then slammed down into the saddle breaking my pelvis. It would have taken hours for a rescue crew with a gurney to arrive and there appeared to be no way for a helicopter to help, so, we managed to get me back on a quieter horse to ride out to the parking lot. Four hours later I was on the surgery table at my home town hospital getting internal body armor (a titanium plate). Healing of a separated pubic symphysis can be a very long-drawn-out process. It only took five years. I have had all the pleasures of childbirth but only a small scar to show for my effort.

I was working cattle and trying to cope with an extremely mad aggressive cow. She chased after me and I managed to escape and hide behind a steel panel gate. She never even slowed down, hit the gate at full speed, and ripped it off the hinges. I was knocked flat on my back on the ground with the gate on top, and her on top of the gate. At least when she tried to grind me into the ground with her head, I was well protected. When the cattleman said, "Sic 'em," to his Blue Healer, the cow only got madder. When she finally decided I was totally dead, she snorted off looking for another target. It took two cowboys to lift the gate off my carcass. I wiped the snot and slobber out of my hair and off my face and went back to work. The gate also survived unscathed except for some manure stains.

To determine if a cow is pregnant, you put her in a cattle squeeze and reach into her rectum and palpate the size, location, and shape of the uterus. It is possible to make a determination at 6 weeks of pregnancy. We aren't as accurate in determining sex and color. It is someone's job to protect you from the next cow in line. The cowboy was dreaming about his girlfriend and I got hit from behind by the head of the next cow and cracked two ribs. When she squeezed past, she spun me along the panels of the alley way like I was a rolling pin. It only hurt when I laughed (for the next three months).

My most potentially serious injury was caused by a horse. I will never admit that it was my own fault. We brought home two horses we purchased in Tennessee. After a few days of letting them get acquainted over the fence we put them together with our three other horses. I was putting out grain tubs one morning being aware that their eagerness for grain combined with a developing pecking order could lead to problems. As I was putting down a tub for the pecking order #4 horse, the #5 horse tried to sneak in and steal a bite. The #4 horse kicked at the #5 horse and got me with a glancing blow to the face instead. Apparently, I managed to get to the house and my wife took me into the hospital. I remember putting the tubs down but have no recollection of the following eight hours. I appeared to be fully conscious to everyone present and was concerned about my contact lenses. When I was finally aware of my surroundings, I asked my son if the doctors had taken them out and he replied with slight exasperation, "Yes Dad, for the 20th time, the doctors took out and saved your contact lenses." The injury straightened out the crook in my nose, and except when sleeping, I have tried to be fully conscious ever since. The contact lenses were found safe in their solution filled container.

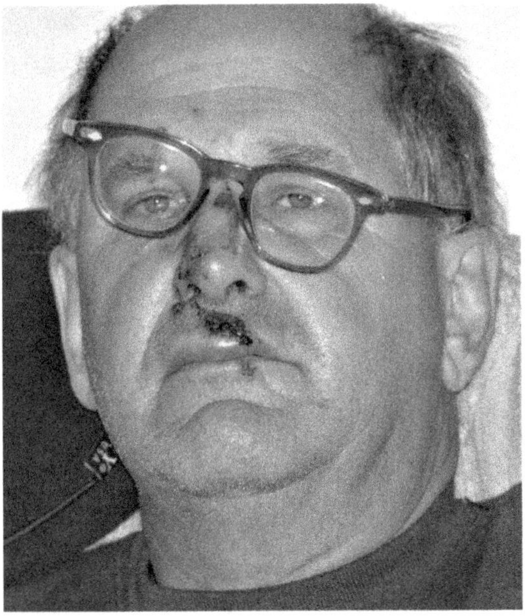

**Doctor Frankenstein's Monster**

# VIGNETTES

**Magic mushrooms**: When I lived in British Columbia in the 1970's, psychedelic mushrooms were in vogue among a certain segment of the population. Local dairy farmers often sprayed on liquid cow manure to fertilize their pastures. This apparently provided the perfect soil environment for the growth of these tiny magic mushrooms. People arrived from California, Florida, Nova Scotia, even Australia carrying maps marking the local fields where these mushrooms could be found. These mushrooms, when dried, were worth $35 an ounce. People crawled on their hands and knees through the manure picking these mushrooms, and in the process let cows out of pastures, bulls were let into pastures, but the dairyman were the ones who were in legal trouble when they over enthusiastically tried to protect their property. Trespass laws were very weak and the pickers would only return the very next day even if the RCMP had become involved. Sensing an unfilled need, I organized meetings at my office for the dairyman, local MLA (members of legislative assembly), and the RCMP where we discussed the issue. It turns out the same problem had been occurring on Vancouver Island as well. We were able to arouse enough political interest that legislation was finally passed giving the property owners more rights on trespass issues.

**Working dogs**: Some younger officers in our local police force decided having a working dog would be a valuable tool in their law enforcement efforts for drug detection or people control. However, funding was tight and their requests seem to be following on deaf ears. So, we started a fundraising campaign and I volunteered to provide any preventive and emergency medical services required by such a dog and encouraged a local feed store to donate necessary food. This stimulated enough local enthusiasm that funds were found and the city has usually had a drug-sniffing or dual-purpose dog on the force ever since. They help track and capture law breakers, sniff for drugs, and respond to the adoring attention of grade school students.

**Fish and wildlife**: Our area is home to a large reintroduced (1913) population of elk. The numbers are high enough that supplemental feed is needed to get the elk through the winters and prevent them from encroaching on agricultural lands. There was a young fish and wildlife officer who was willing to put in time and effort above and beyond that which his job required. In one case elk were dying in greater than usual numbers in one of these supplements feeding locations. He and I examined some of these carcasses and determined that they were dying of pneumonia. In any meat animal such as poultry, pork, or beef, if confined too closely, stress and the concentration of disease elements often show up as pneumonia. This appeared to be the case here and we may have lessened the problem by scattering the feed over a wider area thus reducing the social and disease pressure on the animals.

Additionally, a spike elk (yearling) was observed apparently in good health but with an arrow protruding from his forehead. We were able to determine his daily walking routine and one morning lay in ambush. With a tranquilizer gun we popped him in the butt and about a minute later he lay down for an unscheduled nap. It took both of us to pull the broad head arrow out of his forehead.

On another occasion an elk had decided that it was safer hiding among a herd of Black Angus cattle. His camouflage was not very effective but he was, in fact, in an area where hunting was prohibited. The elk was not being particularly disruptive but the cattleman complained wanting the animal removed. Again, we lay in ambush and darted the elk and eventually hauled it about 30 miles away where we hoped it would join another herd. It only took 5 days for the elk to rejoin its adopted extended family of Black Angus cattle.

**Evil people**: There was a very distressing spate of dead cats found in local neighborhood alleys. One of my detective friends on the police force and the animal control officer contacted me to see if we could determine what was happening. When I examined the bodies, they all had major blunt force trauma to their heads. These were not sick animals, accidental deaths, or animals having been hit by a car. I surmised that some horrible person had caught the unfortunate cats and swing them around by their legs until their head struck something hard. Several weeks later two individuals,14 and 17 years old, were caught breaking off car antennas. They were asked if they had been killing cats as well and they mockingly answered "Yes." The older boy had been coercing the younger boy to perform these horrible acts. At that time cruelty to animals was only a misdemeanor and not a felony. Thus, they were never arraigned for this miserable deed but were prosecuted for property damage. I have often wondered if these two psychopaths graduated to prison for some even more heinous crime such as murder.

**Nursing Home**: My family doctor called one day saying that one of his patients was moving into an extended care nursing facility. He inquired as to what we might do with her pet dog (a sweet Cavalier King Charles Spaniel). I suggested that the dog go with her and he replied that the nursing home administrator would not allow it. I suggested we go talk to her and convince her to change her mind. When we had that conversation, we were pretty much stonewalled because she felt it would disrupt the other patients and an animal might bring diseases into the facility. She was adamant and could not be persuaded. I found articles that discussed zoonosis and the fact that pets usually have different bacterial flora than do people. I also asked if we couldn't at least bring the dog in for a visit. She reluctantly agreed to that low-level commitment. I took the dog in several times always making sure it was carefully controlled and well-groomed. On the fourth or fifth such visit I accidentally on purpose let the dog loose and it wandered from room to room visiting all the other residents who were delighted by the attention from this friendly pet. Eventually we convinced the administrator that the dog could have a trial stay and I said if it didn't work out that I would be responsible. Very quickly the dog became so popular with the other residents that it was designated an honorary permanent staff member. The nursing staff eagerly volunteered to essentially be voluntary pet control officers for a portion of each day.

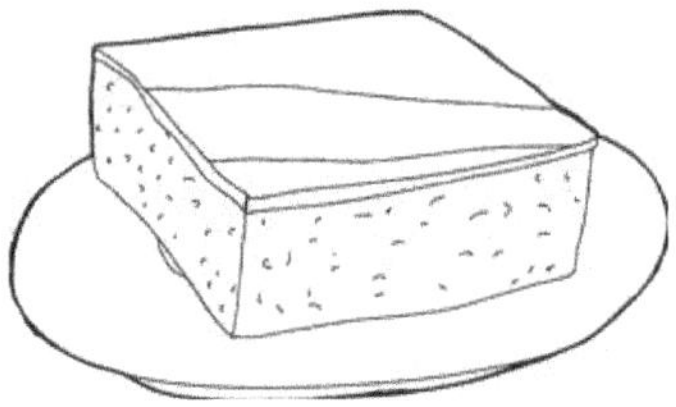

# A 'MOSTLY TRUE' STORY

The old lady was a pet hoarder. She preferred cats but had dogs, horses, donkeys, goats, emus, turkeys, ducks, geese, potbellied pigs, etc. You name it and she probably had a few. But they were mostly rescues and were all well cared for. When they needed attention, she brought them in to us for treatment. Sometimes it seemed that she took better care of the animals than she did of herself. She was always clean but her hair and clothes showed signs of hard use and little care. She always had a large outstanding bill in spite of the fact we gave her major discounts. We knew she was providing homes for otherwise unwanted animals so we were glad to help out as best we could.

From time to time, in an effort to keep her financial fences well mended, she brought in goodies for us as a token of her appreciation. They could be vegetables or fruit when in season or cookies or brownies. Her specialty, however, was fudge. The staff especially like this treat until it was discovered there was a high density of roughage included in the fudge. Most of the cats lived indoors and were, of course, everywhere: on the furniture, tables, and counters; the very same counters she used for preparation of the delicious fudge. We started calling it 'hairy fudge'. The candy lovers on the staff ate the fudge nevertheless, but we jokingly said that they needed hair clippers to cut the fudge and cat hairball medicine for afterwards. No dental flossing was needed after eating this special treat.

In time, all pets age and eventually reach a point where the end is near. Such was the case with an old gray mama cat. The old lady especially loved all her cats and we occasionally had to nudge her in the direction of an appropriate and timely end as they failed. She hated to give up on them. This cat was 20 or 21 years old and there wasn't much left but hair, skin, and bones.

The old lady called one Saturday evening and said, "I know the end is near for old Mama Cat, but isn't there something we can do to keep her going a little bit longer?" I somewhat reluctantly agreed to see the cat knowing that it would only add to the bill that she struggled to pay and that there was little hope for the old cat.

We put her on a blanket on the examination table. You had to look closely to make sure she was still breathing. The stethoscope revealed the faint flutter of a failing heart. She said, "My husband is out of town for the weekend and he wanted to be able to say goodbye. Can't we do something to tide her over until Monday?"

I said, "We can keep her warm and give her fluids."

She asked, "Isn't there something we can do to stimulate her appetite. You've been doing this sort of work for such a long time. Surely you must have some old tricks up your sleeve that we could try." I tried to avoid the inevitable but finally reluctantly agreed to a last-ditch effort.

I knew an old veterinarian who practiced here in the valley in the 1930s, 40s, and 50s and saw him once give a small dose of turpentine to a sick cow. I had serious doubts but never the less agreed to try a similar approach to old Mama Cat.

I didn't have any turpentine but did have a little bit of lawn mower gas. I went out to the shed behind the clinic and pulled about 1/2 cc of gasoline into a small syringe. I eased a feeding tube down the kitty's esophagus into the stomach and administered the small dose. The effect was most startling! First, the whiskers and eyebrows started twitching. Then, little by little, tremors spread down through the whole body. Finally, the kitty raised its head up off the table and blinked at us with a dazed look on her face. This lasted for about 30 seconds when suddenly she jumped up, flew off the table, and ricocheted around the room. She finally slowed down and collapsed in the middle of the room. She lay there breathing heavily, lifted her head once more to look around, and dramatically fell over dead.

We stood there stupefied for about a minute until the old lady finally said, "What just happened?"

I said, "I'm not sure since I have never tried this treatment before, but I think she just ran out of gas."

# POPCORN TURKEY

This favorite special old family recipe has been handed down through a long line of Thanksgiving gourmands but I have updated it to utilize contemporary cooking techniques and appliances.

It is important to select and reserve a fresh unfrozen turkey from your favorite butcher. Freezing alters the texture of the meat at a cellular level and leaves the breast meat dryer and tougher. Examine your bird well in advance. Tom versus hen doesn't seem to matter nor does the size. Check for any missed pin feathers or filoplumes (hair feathers) remaining in the skin which are easily removed with needle nosed pliers. (We used to singe them off with a wad of rolled up flaming newspaper). Rinse and check the cavities for any unwanted undesirable remnants and then carefully dry with a clean white cotton dish towel.

The key to this recipe is dry brine. Some recipes use wet brine where the turkey is soaked overnight in strong salt water solution but this approach leaves the skin saturated and less crispy when cooked. Other recipes use kosher or sea salt but this recipe calls for movie theater flavored popcorn salt. Put the turkey in a plastic bag, add up to one cup of popcorn salt, seal the bag, and then shake to assure that all surfaces of the turkey inside and out are well coated with the salt mixture. Put the bagged turkey in a cold environment (less than 40 degrees) for 24 - 48 hours. The salt brine will pull much of the moisture out to the surface but the concentrated juices will be reabsorbed into the meat when cooking begins leading to maximum juiciness.

Cooking time can be extensive depending on the size of the turkey so be sure to start early enough on Thanksgiving morning depending on the size of your bird. Remove the turkey from the cooler, extract it from the bag, and let it warm to room temperature. Shake off any remaining excess salt. Most will be dissolved by the turkey juices. Now stuff the cavities, front and back, full with popcorn. Pack firmly. The giblets can be left in the chest cavity if you choose and even the neck can be inverted back into the hole or alternately these parts can be saved for turkey soup. Suture both the chest and abdominal cavities closed with cotton string. Using more string, strap the wings and drumsticks tight against the body to prevent them from overcooking and drying.

Place the bird in a covered roasting pan or oven bag and into the preheated oven. (Use a cool oven at 300 - 325 degrees.) Cooking time is standard based on bird weight (typically 3 - 6 hours). You can now proceed with pumpkin pie, Jell-O fruit salad, green bean casserole, mashed potatoes, candied sweet potatoes, dinner rolls, and other favorite traditional family dishes while the bird cooks.

The magical beauty of this recipe is that you don't even need a meat thermometer. You can tell when the turkey is perfectly cooked because when the meat reaches the ideal critical temperature the popcorn pops and blows the turkey's ass off.

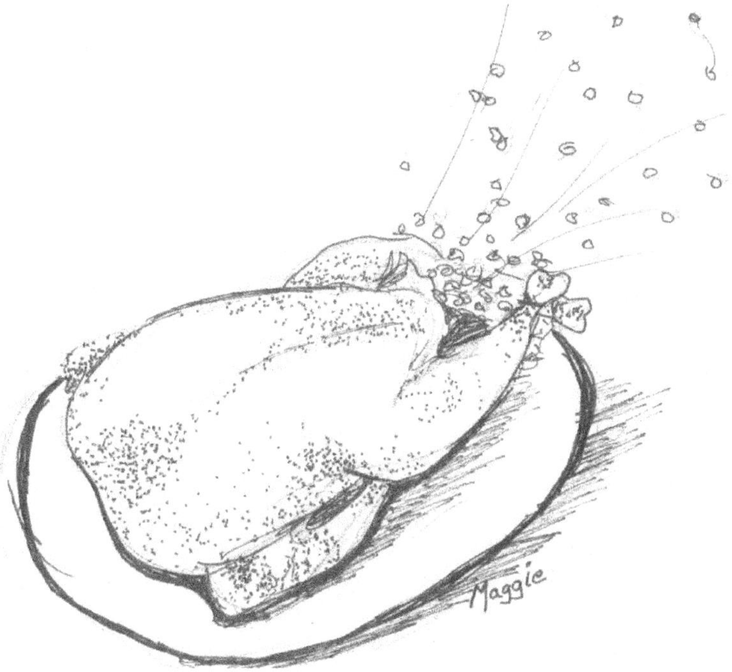

# HOW THE ANGEL GOT ON TOP OF THE CHRISTMAS TREE

Santy wuz sprawled out there in front of the fake 'lectric fireplace watchin RFD TV (with occasional sneaky peeks at the Victoria Secrets Fashion Show), in his green Naugahyde Lazy Boy recliner with his boots off, feet up, and big toes gaspin' for air outa the holes in his wool socks. The chair had permanent impressions that matched Santy's fanny and was a little tattered in front with the stuffin' pokin' out where the barn tom cat had worked it over. Suddenly he jumped up and pulled his time piece out of that special pocket in his Wranglers. "My Gawd. It's 'leven thirty." It wuz Christmas Eve and he had to hit the road by twelve or he wouldn't get all the toys delivered on time to all them good little cowboys and cowgirls.

The cow dog, barn cat, house chicken, dust bunnies, and a few mice scattered when he jumped up, knocked the chair over backwards, and lumbered back to the mud room, groaning as his lumbago kicked in. He dumped everything in the closet out ina pile lookin' for his red Carhartt suit. He shook the moth balls outta the sleeves and stuffed his legs down inta the leg holes. There was a great big RIIIIPPP! The dog barked and checked under his tail to make sure he hadn't done it. Santy lined his backside up agin the mirror and found he had tore the ass end plumb out of them britches. He glanced at his watch and it was 25 to twelve. So, he skinned off them britches and run 'em down to the little tailor elves and said, "Boys, sew these back up!" Usin' bailing twine and some used red cinnamon flavored dental floss, they did.

Santy come in and throwed on his coat and rooted around in the closet fer his boots. He couldn't find 'em 'n holler'd, "Maw! Where's my boots at?"

She was going through the change and said. "Ya damn fool. They're out on the back porch where you left 'em when ya come in last Christmas." An' shurnuff, he hobbled out on the back porch they'd scabbed onto the trailer house, 'n' there they wuz. He'd pulled 'em off soggy last year and they'd dried out all curled up like a possum's tail. He scraped off the white mold and stuffed his feet down in 'em an' dadgum, if the sole didn't fall off of the left boot. He stood there in just his boot top and holey sock with his mouth hanging open. It was a wonder he didn't lose his Copenhagen chew. Santy stared at his watch and it were 20 to twelve.

He ripped them boots off and took 'em down to the little cobbler elves and said. "Boys, hammer this back on!" Using rusty horseshoe nails, they did.

Santy grabbed the pull tabs, yanked on his boots, and run inta the house. He grabbed his coat off the moose antlers, pulled on his cowboy hat with the ear flaps and stampede string (after he dumped out the packrat nest), and took out across the barnyard to hook up the sleigh. The yard light wuz busted and somebody'd left the fresno parked in the middle of the turnaround. He nailed that sucker with his shin bone at a high lope an' flew across the yard ass over teakettle. He hit like a sack of rotten spuds and let out a great big war whoop which stampeded the reindeer an' they went out over the top rail into the summer fallow and scattered into the blackness of the blizzard. Santy grimaced at his watch an' it wuz a quarter 'til twelve!

The little cowboy elves saddled up and brought the reindeer back inta the barn. The toothless Blue Heeler pretty much just barked and got in the way. The head wrangler elf said, "Randolf got a case of the Red Nose and Blister got into the Blue Coat and got a mouth full of Blue Tongue so we'll have to cut 'em out of the hitch."

"OK," said Santy. "Cut out the pregnant ones and the gummers and see if you can find another pair." Somebody'd left the lid off the grain bin and they wuz a little green behind, but they put 'em in the hitch anyway and hooked 'em up to the sleigh. Santy had spent a little too much time at the feed trough in the off season so when he jumped up onto the buckboard seat it busted into kindlin' so they fetched a half rotten bale o'straw fer him to pile his carcass on. Santy climbed aboard agin, cracked the whip 'n' the reindeer took off ina cloud of faintly green exhaust….and Santy just sat there with a silly grin on his face. It were hard fer him to say, "HO! HO! HO!" The rusted runners had froze fast in the muddy ruts and the tugs had busted on the harness! Santy glared at his watch. It were 10 till twelve.

Santy said "Boys, gather up them reindeer again and I'll mend the harness." The leather punch was rusty and wouldn't cut but he cobbled things back together somehow using a knotted shoelace and the leather punch blade on his favorite Boy Scout knife. Then he hitched the team back up, heaved himself into the sleigh, and drove on down in front of the house. Just as they pulled up to the porch, one of the runners fell off the sleigh. "Shit," said Santy. It were 5 till twelve.

"We cain't drive the stone boat. It's full of rocks. I cain't use the John Deere manure spreader. It's full of reindeer crap. We'll have to fix this heap up." So, they drug the sleigh down to the little mechanic elves shop and found some rusty hay "*wore*" behind the barn to lash the runner back on. Santy run into the house. He gave Maw a grumpy peck on the cheek, grabbed that big bag o' toys, and slung 'em over his shoulder…And Yup, you guessed it. The packrats had chewed a hole and the bottom fell outa that bag and toys wus spread out across three counties!

Santy wuz down on his hands and knees, wiping his drippy nose on his dirty sleeve, grubbin' around an' pokin' them toys inta a Safeway shopping bag when a pretty little blond angel come flyin' in the front door in a cloud of snow and a blast of frigid air with a Christmas tree slung over her shoulder. She said "HEY, FAT BOY. Where do you want me to stick this here tree?"

And THAT'S how the pretty little angel got on top of the Christmas tree

Maggie
17

# AFRICAN HORSE SAFARI

What do you do if you are awakened in your tent in the middle of the night by the crash of a nearby tree being uprooted, or huge limbs being ripped off, the roar of a lion close by, or the cackle of a hyena? Simple! You get out of bed, pull on your pants, unzip the tent fly, and walk out in the total darkness to the outhouse. Having taken care of matters, you repeat the process in reverse order and go back to sleep. If, however, you are from LA, London or Manhattan it might be more problematic. It's just another usual night in the veldt of southern Africa.

If you are a truly adventuresome person and an accomplished horseman, there is one unique equine adventure that you shouldn't miss. It is the Limpopo Horse Safari in the south African country of Botswana. I have spent countless days with horses on pack trips in the Cascade Mountains but this trip provides all the exciting wild adventures of Africa, but little of the work. There is truly nothing like it in the world. The downside is that it is 24 hours from Seattle to Johannesburg South Africa with a nine-hour jet lag time difference. You can spend a day or two in Joberg just to adjust to the time difference. While there you can visit the Apartheid Museum, Nelson Mandela's house, and Soweto. From Johannesburg, you then take a four-hour van or one-hour small plane flight north into the southeast corner of Botswana called the Tuli block, which is located at the intersection of South Africa, Zimbabwe, and Botswana just north of the Limpopo River.

Cecil Rhodes was an imperialist British businessman, politician, and mining magnet in southern Africa and was the founder of the De Beers diamond company as well as the provider of the endowment funding for the most prestigious Rhodes Scholarship Program. His British South African Company established the territory of Rhodesia, which has since been divided into Zimbabwe and Zambia. As the Cape Colony prime minister in the 1890s, he championed the concept of building a railroad from Cape Town to Cairo and for this effort was granted rights to a portion of territory which is now southeastern Botswana. The railroad proved to be an impossible engineering feat in this terrain and local tribal Chiefs had to petition the Queen to regain title to the area. It has since fallen into private ownership and it has been found that its greatest value lies with tourism. Today it remains in surprisingly pristine condition with large herds of native wildlife. There is enough rainfall in these highlands (16” to 18”) that the herds do not have to migrate and are present all year around.

Botswana is a democratic country of only 2.25 million people but is the size of France. Through mining, cattle, and tourism they have one of the highest standards of living in Africa. The Botswanan government has banned big game hunting on public lands but there is still limited hunting on some private reserves. There is no hunting except by camera allowed in the Tuli block. Companies are allowed to do tours with fifteen vehicles permitted to drive and observe in an area the size of Kittitas County in Washington State (about 2400 square miles).

At the end of the flight to the Limpopo Valley Airfield, we did a flyover to make sure that no big game was on the landing strip. The safari headquarters had corrals and barns surrounded by 12 ft.

high catproof fences. The horse facilities were patrolled by Rhodesian Ridgebacks which are famous for being the *lion dog* of South Africa. We met the other riders (8 total from UK, France and northern Europe) and after a snack at the Safari headquarters, we changed into our riding habit (boots, breeches and helmets) and were introduced to our horses. They matched us to a horse based on our riding resume and then we took a riding test before we could proceed. The test included handling obstacles you might encounter in the veldt such as brush, ditches, and logs and on a horse you had never ridden before. Not everyone passes. It also involved riding your horse away from the group and then coming back at a full gallop to prove you could control your horse. There were some thoroughbreds and English warmbloods but the predominant horse was a Boerperd (farmer's horse in Dutch/Africans). They are a hardy breed derived from animals brought in by the Dutch settlers in the 1600s which has been refined and developed and has similarities to the Morgan horse. The main camp had about 50 horses with one third on safari, one third resting from their previous weeks work, and one third in training to prepare for safari the following week. There was also a local *troop* of baboons that checked manure piles for any goodies and cleaned up any grain left by the horses.

Then our real adventure began. Eight of us with two guides rode each day to a new tent camp. The camp had a cook and an assistant and five grooms who helped to move and set up the camp and also care for the horses. The two guides also served as the social directors, barmen, and naturalists. We rode typically single file with a guide in front and a guide behind. The lead guide had a large caliber rifle in a scabbard and a bull whip tied to his saddle. He said that the big cats feared the whip mainly because of its loud *crack*. Because there were motor vehicles in the area who communicated by radio, we knew where the dangerous animals were on a particular day and actually during the day attempted, if possible, to avoid them. We did do vehicle game drives in the evening where we were able to see lions, cheetahs, and leopards at very close range.

Our guides woke us well before daylight with our hot drink of choice and we moved to the campfire area for a hot breakfast. The grooms knew each horse well and had them saddled and ready for us to ride out as soon as it was light enough to see. We traveled 15 to 20 miles a day. If you proceeded at a walk it could be a very long day, so, we galloped whenever possible. You could not gallop through thick brush for fear of startling a large predator or elephant or through some grassy areas where elephants walking during the wet season had left huge deep footprints. But when the terrain and habitat allowed, we galloped hard for five to six minutes jumping over occasional logs and across suddenly appearing ditches. The terrain was very reminiscent of central Washington with its African veldt and basalt outcroppings. There were lots of dry stream beds which would be full of water during the rainy season. During the winter when we rode, they appeared dry but actually had water flowing underground which appeared intermittently in large pools. Elephants dug holes in the sand of the river channels which would fill with water for the elephants and other opportunistic animals.

A truck was the kitchen and it also carried our personal gear to the next camp along dirt tracks in the veldt. Each camp had a well, a gravity fed water system, a bucket shower, and outhouses or even flush toilets. A solar powered electric fence was put up at night with the grooms taking turns patrolling the perimeter of the camp.

We did see big cats at a distance during the daytime but tried to avoided disrupting them. We did see a leopard with a kill up in a tree and saw cheetahs out hunting in the daytime. On our evening game drives in Toyota safari trucks, we saw *prides* of lions, 'coalitions' of cheetahs, and *leaps* of leopards. We paused just at dusk one evening when we realized we had driven in among a *pride* of lions, stalking a *confusion* of wildebeests. The lions moved one at a time in an organized choreographed fashion but ultimately the wildebeest escaped. We also saw a leopard hiding just under the lip of a riverbank as a flock of guinea fowl approached. When they flew overhead, he leaped in the air almost catching a bird in midflight about 10 feet off the ground.

We saw a strange impression in the soft soil, like the wobbly track left by a bicycle. Our guide said it was a rock python and I suggested that since we were ahead of schedule we ought to track it. He agreed and we followed it across sandy areas through the grass and brush and finally someone said, "Look! There it is." It was about 10 ft. long and appeared to be sleeping. The sleep was permanent for it was dead. The guide said it had been attacked and killed by a *business* of mongooses who had partially eaten it. They would probably return at dusk that evening to finish their meal. Nothing goes to waste in Africa.

We usually carefully galloped single file but if there was wide enough space the guide allowed us to spread out in a wide front where we could jump logs, bushes, and ditches. The horses absolutely loved what they were doing and decided this was a great time to race especially if we were close to the next camp. Some of the smaller ladies definitely had their hands full keeping the horse under control under these exciting circumstances.

On one occasion as we were galloping we found that we were headed right towards a *parade* of elephants. We couldn't ride behind them because there was a river bank and they were stretched forward over such a long distance, it would have been a major detour to ride around in front of them. The guide was momentarily uncertain just what we should do until a gap developed in the middle of the herd. He explained quietly that we would gallop single-file through this gap but not every rider heard these instructions. Since we were about a half a mile from the next camp and the riders let the horses spread out, the race was on. Three horses were diving towards two gaps between the bushes. One horse thus got squeezed out and had to slam on the brakes. The rider managed to hug her horse's neck on the way off but nevertheless hit the ground and rolled into an acacia bush. When we got to camp it took an hour to pull out all the acacia thorns from her back and shoulder. She was nevertheless none the worse for wear.

I have always ridden in a western saddle but the safari was done in English saddles. It was exciting to discover that at the young age of 74, I still had the skill and balance to ride with just my legs and not with a hand firmly grasping the saddle horn.

Our intent was to not disrupt or stress any animals. One morning as we were on an extended gallop we overtook a small *herd* of impalas and they bounded alongside. Then we encountered a *dazzle* of zebras and they joined in as well. We were smiling and enjoying this evolving situation when we encountered a *journey* or *tower* of giraffes who joined in traveling just as fast, only taking one stride to our six. The zebras gallop much like donkeys while the impalas take 35-foot-long leaps and fly six or seven feet in the air. We eventually slowed to a walk so as not to further disrupt the animals. These wild herds seemed to have joined our gallop of their own volition.

Evenings we ate meals by lantern light prepared over an open fire. After dinner on our first night out I went to my tent and sat down on the bed. There was a strange lump under the blankets and I reached in to discover what it was. I jerked my hand back out in shock when I encountered a hot water bottle. It was winter time and the night temperatures were down into the high 30s. The next morning one of the guests who was in her early twenties and was an excellent rider having done three-day eventing, explained that she was afraid to leave her tent to go to the nearby outhouse during the middle of the night. "I was afraid I was going to wet my bed." There were many strange exotic very dangerous sounding animal noises during the night and she didn't want to get eaten. The guides explained in the morning that the unfamiliar sounds were actually *troops* of baboons and a *cackle* of hyenas that were patrolling the perimeter. That same morning, we had a change of breakfast menu because in the middle of the night a troop of baboons raided the kitchen and stole some of the prepared breakfast fruit.

One night as one of the grooms was out checking on the horses he encountered a large snake and called us all over to see it. It proved to be a black mamba which was very lethargic since it was midwinter. The black mamba has a necro toxin in its bite which will destroy the flesh that has been envenomated. Failure to get antivenom can result in the loss of an extremity due to the tissue damage.

On another night nobody really got much sleep as a *memory* of elephants was feeding in the brush all around the camp. You could hear the crash and snap as they knocked down mopane (mopani) trees and ripped off the branches. They consume leaves, twigs, and branches up to the diameter of your thumb. There is enough cellulose debris in their manure that it can be treated and used to make crude artisan paper. Elephants only extract about 45% of the nutrients from the roughage they consume and therefore eat two to six hundred pounds a day and drink 50 gallons of water.

Other interesting highlights: 1. A giraffe has a twenty-inch tongue so it can pluck green acacia leaves from among the two-inch acacia thorns. We saw a giraffe scratching his butt on an acacia bush, but very carefully. 2. Mashatu trees are massive with an umbrella covering a 150 ft. circle. We camped under one which was also a feeding area for vervet monkeys. They picked the mashatu fruit but spit out the green ones on our heads. 3. We stumbled upon a lion nursery of nine relatively mature lion cubs. The mothers were apparently out hunting. When they heard a call inaudible to us the cubs all got up and traveled to where the mothers had made a kill. 4. Elephants can have up to six sets of teeth which can each last up to ten years. When the last set are worn out the elephant eventually starves to death. We came across the remains of an elephant which had died of old age and only about one third of the bony skull remained. The rest had been eaten by hyenas. Hyenas have massive jaws that can crush even elephant bones and a digestive system that dissolves the consumed bone. There were many piles of hyena poop in the area which looked like formed piles of white chalk. 5. The guides pointed out the carcass of a giraffe that had been killed by lions because it suffered a broken leg. Only part of a femur and the pelvis were left with which the hyenas were playing a very serious game of tug of war. A jackal sneaked in and stole a scrap but reconsidered when the hyenas pursued it. 6. We climbed a basalt outcropping overlooking the vast African plains for a sundowner (traditional gin & tonic evening cocktail). There was a massive baobab tree where the initials of Cecil John Rhodes carved in 1893 were visible.

We saw almost all the animals indigenous to that part of Africa: impala, kudu, eland, giraffe, wildebeest, zebra, lions, cheetahs, leopards, ostrich, jackal, hyena, baboons, vervet monkeys, wart hogs, steenbok, bush buck, water buck, bat eared fox, elephant shrew, hyrax, rock hare, various bats, meerkat, civet cat, guinea fowl, cape mourning doves, tawney eagle, yellow billed hornbill, beautiful lilac breasted roller, weaver birds, split tailed starling, Burchell sage grouse, martial eagle, eagle owl, kori bustard, Egyptian goose, black mamba, rock python, and sand snake. We did not see the dangerous water buffalo, hippo, or rhinoceros.

**This was the trip of a lifetime: *Africa up close and personal.***

LIMPOPO
HORSE SAFARI

# THE FABLE OF THE COYOTE'S TALE

Oral and written tradition by ancient peoples through storytelling, song, dance, carving, and drawing has brought forward fables of many things found in the natural world: animals, mountain ranges, genesis, natural disasters, unnatural events, etc. All Native American tribes seem to have stories about Coyote in their traditional oral history. He can be represented as the trickster, the sly one, the hunter, and even the teacher who passes moral wisdom and judgement to mankind.

Is there some secret coyote DNA hidden in the tissue of Piper my border collie mix? It certainly seems likely when you watch her hunt field mice in the horse pasture. Her nose guides her unerringly towards her target, she pauses to listen, and then leaps straight up in the air coming down trying to trap the vole beneath her sensitive paws. She certainly is an excellent hunter but obviously passes judgment down on me when I am late with her kibble dinner.

This is the fable of ***The Coyote's Tail*** as passed down through countless generations of tribal elders from time immemorial.

Back in the days before man ascended, the world was a much simpler place. The earth was untouched by war and political strife. The animal world of North America was partitioned into various Clans: The Grazing Clan - the buffalo, horses, antelope, deer, and the elk, The Cat Clan – cougar, lynx, and the bobcat, The Bird Clan - the raven, migrating song birds, the grouse family, hawks, owls, and the eagle, The Fur Bearing Animals – mink, martin, beaver, otter, and wolverine, and of course The Canine Clan - the wolf, fox, and the coyote. Each clan typically gathered every decade or so to sort out political and social issues of mutual concern.

This was the case with the Canine Clan. They gathered together in midwinter to discuss important issues of potential conflict such as hunting territory and rules for communication. They didn't want to poach on other members hunting territory or go around marking the wrong trees. They assembled high in the mountains at a secret gathering place of giant caves left from the days of ancient vulcanization. Stealing fire from an active volcano, they built a huge bonfire in the largest cave. Representatives from the Wolves and the Foxes were there in large numbers.

Coyote, however, was a loner and not very social beyond the boundaries of his own Clan. One winter he arrived late as usual, but was uncertain whether he wanted to attend that year. He skulked around outside listening to the growling, howling, barking, yipping and yapping inside in the flickering light of the giant fire. Next to the giant cave was a smaller cave that was used like a hatcheck room. Only in this case it was for checking tails. Tails are one of the Canine Clan's best means of long-distance silent communication and fearing that wrong signals might be given in the middle of heated discussion, it was customary to check tails before entering the giant cave so as to avoid possible misunderstandings or miscommunication. At the last possible moment before the meeting began Coyote decided he would not participate that year. But he felt he needed to leave some mark or indication that he had been present. So, he ducked into the tail check room and totally rearranged all the tails putting them on different hooks. Grinning slyly and feeling smug and very pleased with himself, he sat back for a moment licking his chops and listening to the babbling from the giant cave.

Just before departing for places unknown, he stuck his head into the giant cave and shouted FIRE! FIRE! Then he hid behind a boulder at the cave's entrance to watch and see what would happen. Of course, all the Wolves and Foxes rushed out of the cave but ducked into the tail check room first to retrieve their tail before scattering.

To this very day all members of the Canine Clan continue sniffing the butts of every other Canine they meet to see if they can find the tail that they lost so many eons ago.

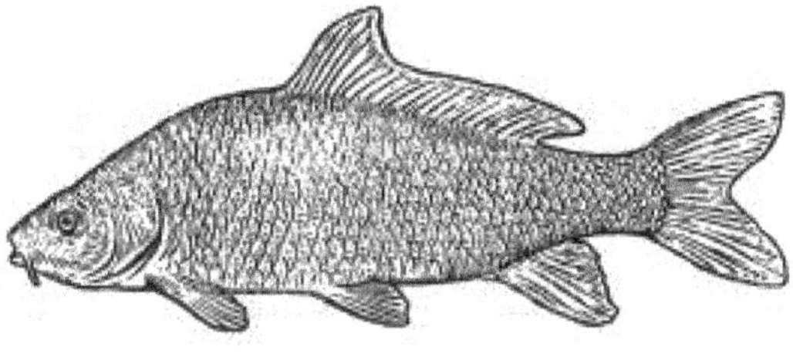

# PLANKED CARP RECIPE

Another ancient recipe from Eastern Europe comes to mind. It is for Planked Carp. Many people consider carp to be a bottom feeder trash fish that is undesirable to eat. It is notoriously boney and the flesh may have muddy flavor. The way to circumvent these problems involves two steps.

First: fillet the fish. This disposes of most of the bones as they are left with the carcass. Once the meat is properly cooked the remaining bones seem to separate out nicely from the flesh.

Second: remove the skin. The muddy flavor comes primarily from the fatty layer beneath the skin. Thus the muddy flavor is overcome.

The next step is appropriate seasoning. This is left to the individual chef's discretion. I prefer Johnny's Seasoning Salt but there are, of course, many commercial seasoning products developed especially for fish. The skinned fish fillet can be put in a baggie with a tablespoon of seasoning and left for an hour to marinade.

The final important item is to select an appropriate small hardwood plank. Cutting boards are typically made from oak or maple and they can serve quite nicely.

The pre-seasoned fish is placed on the plank and appropriate number of bacon strips are placed on top to cover most of the top surface. This will add flavor and prevent the flesh from drying.

Finally the planked fish and bacon are placed in a cool oven, about 300 degrees for 40 to 50 minutes. You can tell when the fish is perfectly cooked because the meat flakes apart nicely with a fork. When you have determined that it is done, you remove the fish and plank from the oven and carefully scrape the fish off with a stainless-steel spatula and into the garbage and eat the plank.

# THE END

# ACKNOWLEDGEMENTS

These stories, with a few self-evident exceptions, all have a foundation in actual events. Names and places have been changed and some literary liberty has obviously been exercised.

Physicians, out of necessity, often deal with people who are in pain, are sick, or have some sort of medical problem making the personal interaction less than ideal. For the most part, veterinarian's dealings with people are positive and hopefully these client's lives can be enriched by addressing a medical problem they have with their animals.

These stories are dedicated to the people and the animals in the daily life of a 'country vet'. The support, inspiration, and encouragement by friends, loved ones, family and pets has been invaluable in completing this enjoyable project. The fine artwork and graphics by Maggie German add their own unique texture and character to the narrative.

My border collie cross Piper was a rescue. I spayed her one day and got both or my hips replaced the following day. This is how I began my retirement. Two weeks later I called to see if she still needed a home and she has been my constant companion ever since. She has kept my feet warm while writing these stories, my fingers flexible for keyboarding from scratching her ears and belly, and my stomach satisfied by sharing the people treats she occasionally requests. She sleeps at my feet as I write these last lines.

**PIPER**